PRIMARY ENGLISH TEACHING: AN INTRODUCTION TO LANGUAGE, LITERACY AND LEARNING

Education at SAGE

SAGE is a leading international publisher of journals, books, and electronic media for academic, educational, and professional markets.

Our education publishing includes:

- accessible and comprehensive texts for aspiring education professionals and practitioners looking to further their careers through continuing professional development

- inspirational advice and guidance for the classroom

- authoritative state of the art reference from the leading authors in the field

Find out more at: **www.sagepub.co.uk/education**

PRIMARY ENGLISH TEACHING: AN INTRODUCTION TO LANGUAGE, LITERACY AND LEARNING

ROBYN COX

Los Angeles | London | New Delhi
Singapore | Washington DC

SAGE Publications Ltd
1 Oliver's Yard
55 City Road
London EC1Y 1SP

SAGE Publications Inc.
2455 Teller Road
Thousand Oaks, California 91320

SAGE Publications India Pvt Ltd
B 1/I 1 Mohan Cooperative Industrial Area
Mathura Road
New Delhi 110 044

SAGE Publications Asia-Pacific Pte Ltd
33 Pekin Street #02-01
Far East Square
Singapore 048763

Library of Congress Control Number: 2010928190

British Library Cataloguing in Publication data

A catalogue record for this book is available from the British Library

ISBN 978-1-84920-195-7
ISBN 978-1-84920-196-4

Typeset by C&M Digitals (P) Ltd., Chennai, India
Printed in Great Britain by MPG Books Group, Bodmin, Cornwall
Printed on paper from sustainable resources

Mixed Sources
Product group from well-managed
forests and other controlled sources
www.fsc.org Cert no. SA-COC-1565
© 1996 Forest Stewardship Council
FSC

CONTENTS

Series published in association with UKLA

The emphasis for all of the books is this series is on developing practical skills for teachers in literacy and language teaching, underpinned by accessibly presented theory and research. Dealing with topics of current and continuing interest, the books aim to inform all those concerned with the development of literacy: teachers, researchers and local authority professionals, as well as those involved in teacher education and continuing professional development.

Books in the series:
Phonics: Practice, Research and Policy Maureen Lewis and Sue Ellis (editors), 2006

Visual Approaches to Teaching Writing: Multimodal Literacy 5–11 Eve Bearne and Helen Wolstencroft, 2007

Desirable Literacies: Approaches to Language and Literacy in the Early Years (Second Edition) Jackie Marsh and Elaine Hallett (editors), 2008

The United Kingdom Literacy Association (UKLA) is a registered charity, which has as its sole object the advancement of education in literacy at all levels and in all educational settings in the UK and overseas. Members include classroom teachers, teaching assistants, school literacy co-ordinators, LEA literacy consultants, teacher educators, researchers, inspectors, advisors, publishers and librarians.

UKLA provides a forum for discussion and debate through a wide range of international, national, regional and local conferences and publications. UKLA works with a range of government and non-governmental agencies on issues of national interest. The Association is also committed to the funding and dissemination of high-quality national and international research projects that include practitioner-researchers. This series of co-published titles with Sage Publications complements the range of in-house UKLA publications and provides a further opportunity to disseminate the high quality work of the association. In order to find out more about UKLA, including details about membership, visit: http://www.ukla.org

FOREWORD

This book is written by lecturers in the field of initial teacher education (ITE) in England and aims to provide a comprehensive introduction to language and learning in the primary school. It makes the assumption that accepted pedagogical practice in the primary English language classroom is not without very strong research-based theoretical roots. By exploring this theory the authors in the chapters have provided a strong theory–practice link for those enrolled in undergraduate and postgraduate ITE programmes. It is the editor and authors' belief that students will be well placed to understand the resultant pedagogical practice and curriculum offerings in English primary schools today.

The book has a series of boxes which aim to allow the reader to explore the research further or undertake a focused task to assist in clarifying the ideas being discussed or giving actual classroom-based teaching ideas:

1 *Research box*. This aims to draw the reader's attention to theoretical aspects underpinning what is being discussed. It is correctly referenced with signposts for further exploration should the reader like to do so.

2 *Task box*. This is a practical university class activity to help readers clarify their thoughts.

3 *Teaching ideas*. This is to provide an opportunity for contributors to bridge the theory–practice divide instantly by drawing the attention of the reader to perhaps: a well-known pedagogical approach; a National Literacy Strategy activity; a useful idea for grouping; or a popular use of a resource. These ideas are 'springboards' only, for the readers to try something out rather than being a prescriptive set of lesson ideas.

The editor and authors have tried very hard to explore and respond to diversity as part of each of the chapters. Similarly aspects of special educational needs are embedded in the specific chapters and contributions.

Chapter 1 is written by the editor, Robyn Cox. It is titled 'Exploring language and learning' and provides some theory about what is currently understood about language acquisition. This chapter also gives an introduction to educational linguistics which ensures that the reader has theory with which to move forward when reading the rest of the book. However, readers may want to 'dip' into sections of this chapter as they read the more curriculum-based chapters that follow.

The next four chapters sit together as they are all about the learning and teaching of literacy in the primary school. Chapter 2, also written by Robyn Cox, provides focus on developmental aspects of language acquisition, research findings and classroom practice in relation to talk in the primary school. Chapter 3, written by Andrew Lambirth, presents a very strong introduction to the theories behind models of teaching reading and, by reading this, ITE students will be well placed to plan for the reader in their primary classrooms. Similarly, Chapter 4 written by Liz Chamberlain provides an insightful view into the teaching of writing together with the theories that inform classroom practice. Chapter 5 is an innovative chapter in an ITE textbook because it is written by Jean Webb, a Professor of Children's Literature, and gives an insight into the literary theory utilized by researchers in the field of Children's Literature. The author makes explicit links to the classroom and calls on the professional teacher to utilize the vast array of books written for children across time and place.

Chapter 6 is about the developing area of information and communication technology (ICT) in the primary literacy curriculum. Written by Bob Fox, it closely focuses on established uses of ICT from the use of interactive white boards to emerging uses such as the use of Wikis and blogs. The next chapter, written by Jane Medwell, introduces the importance of handwriting to the literacy learner. Jane combines this with ideas about typing and keyboard skills. This is an innovative presentation of a topic rarely given much focus in recent books written for ITE.

Chapter 8, again written by Jane Medwell, is a very strong discussion about assessment in English in the primary school. Medwell investigates the broad area of assessment to provide a strong base for assessment in the primary English curriculum. Jane expertly presents current debates in the area and calls upon the reader to engage in the wider research into assessing English literacy. Chapter 9 is a very strong chapter about planning for the English classroom. It is written by Carrie Ansell and provides some practical ideas for planning which are situated in the theoretical framework of the inclusive classroom. The chapter focuses on planning, which is much more than simply differentiation. The final chapter is unusual in that it presents the life journey of a primary English teacher. Written by Chris Robertson, the chapter documents the journey from a teacher of reading in a primary school to Professor of Education and Head of the Institute of Education, and suggests that those in teacher education have rich backgrounds and can be seen as taking a 'stewardship' role in ITE in England in these 'changing times'.

CONTRIBUTORS

Carrie Ansell is a Senior Lecturer in primary and early years English at Bath Spa University, where she is presently course co-ordinator. She has worked in primary education for over 20 years, primarily in primary schools which had a multilingual and culturally diverse population. Her main research interests are in the field of linguistic diversity and bilingualism.

Liz Chamberlain is a Senior Lecturer at the University of Winchester and co-ordinates English across the faculty. She is also the Strategic Consultant for Everybody Writes, a project concerned with exploring writing beyond the classroom and getting pupils excited about writing by offering them real audiences for their writing. Her PhD interest is in children's attitudes to writing, shared understandings, and how different writing approaches and pedagogies are implemented in primary classrooms.

Robyn Cox is Associate Professor at the Australian Catholic University and a member of the executive committee of the United Kingdom Literacy Association (UKLA; www.ukla.org). She is the author of several international journal articles in the field of literacy research and has been involved in teacher education in four countries over a 20-year period. Robyn is well known for her commitment to the development of a strong professional knowledge base in initial teacher education.

Bob Fox has been a primary teacher, a head teacher, an advisory teacher and a university lecturer, training teachers in the effective use of ICT. He is the author of various books, academic papers and conference presentations on ICT-related matters. He has recently retired as e-learning co-ordinator in the Institute of Education at the University of Worcester.

Andrew Lambirth is Professor at Greenwich University, London. Before joining higher education, he was a primary school teacher in Peckham and Bermondsey in South-East London. Andrew has published widely in the field of the teaching of literacy and English. His latest book is to be called *Literacy of the Left*. He is well known for his interest in sociocultural, class and political perspectives on education and the teaching of literacy.

Jane Medwell teaches PGCE and early childhood studies in the Institute of Education, University of Warwick. She has been a lecturer in other universities and a teacher in primary schools. She has conducted research in effective teachers of literacy, information technology (IT) and literacy, writing and handwriting as well as teacher education.

Chris Robertson is Professor and Head of the University of Worcester's highly successful Institute of Education which she has led from strength to strength since her appointment. In the most recent Ofsted inspection of primary education, for example, an outstanding outcome and report was achieved, noting both outstanding teacher training provision and outstanding management and quality leading to the highest possible grade. She has continued to lead her large institute with creativity, imagination and vision, and always with a strong focus on achieving the best for children. Chris has a very strong professional and academic commitment to issues of inclusion and social justice in education. Her commitment to making a real difference to the learning and lives of all children has been a constant theme throughout her long career.

Jean Webb is Professor of International Children's Literature at the University of Worcester where she is also Director of the International Centre for Research in Children's Literature, Literacy and Creativity. Her publications include: with Deborah Cogan Thacker, *Introducing Children's Literature: Romanticism to Postmodernism* (London, Routledge, 2000); 'The real and the child-like: generation and philosophy in Tove Jansson's *The Summer Book*', in *Tove Jansson Rediscovered*, K. McLoughlin and M. Lindström Brock (eds) (CSP, 2007); 'Voracious appetites: the construction of "fatness" in children's literature', in *Food in Children's Literature: Critical Approaches*', Kara Keeling and Scott Pollard (eds) (Routledge 2009); and 'Aesthetic hegemony: Western scholars and Native American culture', in *What Do You See? International Perspectives on Children's Book Illustration*', Jennifer Harding and Pat Pinsent (eds) (CSP, 2008).

ACKNOWLEDGEMENTS

The editor and publisher would like to thank the following for permission to use figures in the book:

Bearne, E. (2002) *Making Progress in Writing*. Reprinted by permission of the publisher (Taylor and Francis Group, http://www.informaworld.com)

Cummins, J. (1984) *Bilingualism and Special Education: Issues in Assessment and Pedagogy*. Reprinted by permission of the publisher Multilingual Matters Publications

Gravelle, M. (2000) *Planning for Bilingual Learners: An inclusive curriculum*. Reprinted by permission of the publisher Trentham Books

CHAPTER 1

EXPLORING LANGUAGE AND LEARNING

ROBYN COX

How do we learn language? Is it the same as how we learn to walk or how we learn to do mathematics? These are the questions that characterize the long theoretical journey by researchers and thinkers which produced the theories of language acquisition which underlie much of the pedagogy of the primary English literacy classroom today. The first section of this chapter outlines the three main language acquisition theories that emerged early in the twentieth century: the behaviourist theory of language acquisition; the cognitivist theory of language acquisition; and the sociocultural theory of language acquisition.

Behaviourist theory of language acquisition

Early work by B.F. Skinner identified that all learning is a result of stimulus response and that people will learn when they are rewarded for their efforts. This grew out of experiments with animals and a growing knowledge of physiology and neural work, and proved to be an adequate explanation for language acquisition and language learning. During this period a number of questions were raised about this view of language learning. Those questions focused on the particularity of humans to learn language so efficiently and if it was as simple as stimulus–response then why could not animals learn to talk. So began a series of experiments across the world to try to teach those animals with physiology similar to that of humans, such as the ape family, and, most famously, chimpanzees, to speak.

Many famous experiments were conducted into primate language research, in particular with chimpanzees, gorillas and orang-utans. However, because non-human primates lack vocal cords and other human speech organs, the experiments often utilized primates' manual dexterity and had them operate keyboards.

It is now generally accepted that apes can learn to sign and are able to communicate with humans. However, it is disputed as to whether they can form syntax to manipulate such signs. The idea that chimps could use the language of symbols but were unable to generate syntax or grammar was what convinced researchers that language is unique to the human species.

Cognitivist theory of language acquisition

During this time another researcher emerged – who felt strongly that it was not as simple as the picture painted by the behaviourists and that there was something very unique about language acquisition. His theory was supported in part by the outcome from the previous animal studies that chimpanzees could not produce 'novel sentences' – or those sentences they had not heard before – which is something that babies can readily accomplish.

Chomsky (1959) thus established that the human species had something which animals did not have which is a language acquisition device (LAD). The argument emerged that language acquisition is specialized learning which is peculiar to humans. Chomsky's theory about language acquisition was based on his idea of the 'novel sentence'. He stated that a young language learner had the ability to create a 'novel sentence', that is, a sentence that they have composed without ever hearing it spoken before. If young language learners only ever repeated what they heard then the swiftness of language acquisition for interaction in toddlers and pre-schoolers would not be possible.

Task box

Spend some time talking with a young child, thinking very carefully about Chomsky's ideas of novel sentences.

Talk to children about something they are doing and ask them a question such as 'Tell me about your game'. I am certain that they will give you the information in bursts of language, words which are linked together but may not be particularly grammatically perfect. The language will be rich with meaning and probably have groups of words put together that this language learner has never put together before.

If you do not think that this will happen, make some notes of the groups of words that they use and then ask the parents, teachers or carers if they have heard the children use this language before.

Make a note of how many words the child uses together. Are there one-word utterances; two-word utterances (what is the function of each of these words – descriptor + name, and so on)?

Sociocultural theory of language acquisition

Chomsky's (1957) work is known as seminal because it changed the way we think about language acquisition and, as a result, language teaching and learning. It began to engage educators in thinking about what might be the best way to provide contexts for babies and children to acquire language. It was not long before this thinking moved into more formal educational contexts and, even, what it might mean for the learning of literacy (the comprehending and composing of written language).

Research into language learning at this time took on a new perspective – the importance of other adults in relation to the child learner took on a rising profile and began the movement of researchers looking at child–adult interaction as the central basis for language acquisition.

The earliest of these child interaction studies resulted in an array of findings – often referred to as child studies – where individual children's learning patterns were extrapolated to the wider population. Following from these strong research beginnings many more practical pedagogical implications emerged and important secondary results came from these studies – most noticeably the child observation instruments which form the basis for many of the currently used National Curriculum levelling moderation processes. Some examples are the ELL project (Pascal and Bertram, 1997), *Biks and Gutches* (Clay, 1990b) and *First Steps* (DEWA, 1999). The identification of the specific language addressed to infants and young children by caregivers become important and a new term was conceived: 'motherese'. Once this was identified, focus moved to making sure that those whose professional duty was working with young children had knowledge of the importance of language play, games and imaginative play.

Michael Halliday's (1975) *Learning How to Mean* presented the rich data and analysis of his own son's first 20 months of language learning. Halliday began what turned out to be his distinguished contribution to the field of linguistics when he noted that language acquisition is indeed a series of choices that the learner makes while learning to interact. He accepted the importance of the LAD, but more importantly he underscored the importance of the role of the interlocutor with the child learner. The identification that the language choices learners made were a result of the functional purpose of the language led him to develop a series of language functions.

One of the results from Halliday's (1975) work was the recognition that children are motivated to acquire language because it serves certain purposes or functions for them. He went so far as to identify these functions, and it is always useful for students seeking to work with young children who are acquiring language to be familiar with these.

The first four functions help the child to satisfy physical, emotional and social needs:

- *Instrumental*. This is when the child uses language to express their needs (for example, 'Want juice').
- *Regulatory*. This is where language is used to tell others what to do (for example, 'Go away').
- *Interactional*. Here language is used to make contact with others and form relationships (for example, 'Love you, mummy').
- *Personal*. This is the use of language to express feelings, opinions and individual identity (for example, 'Me good girl').

The next three functions help the child to come to terms with his or her environment:

- *Heuristic*. This is when language is used to gain knowledge about the environment (for example, 'What is the dog doing?').
- *Imaginative*. Here language is used to tell stories and jokes, and to create an imaginary environment.
- *Representational*. The use of language to convey facts and information.

At the same time an increased focus on children learning two languages either at the same time (simultaneously) or one after the other (consecutively) became apparent and a body of literature emerged which presented case studies of bilingualism in children. This growing area of research became known as studies in bilingualism and generated a range of theories and pedagogical practices. It was the recognition of the rich linguistic background of some children entering school that led to, what this writer believes to be, the most famous 10 words ever written about language and education. These words were conceived by the team who produced the Bullock Report – the first enquiry into the teaching of English conducted internationally and commissioned by the then Department of Education in the UK. These words were: 'No child should leave their language at the classroom door' (DES, 1975: 45).

These famous words were to make an impact on the teaching of English in primary classrooms across the world, but unfortunately in the UK in the early 2000s it may be thought that these words have been forgotten. The work of early childhood researchers and theorists has ensured that these words have been enshrined in the Foundation Stage Curriculum materials but in Key Stage 1 and Key Stage 2 what has happened? We leave this discussion to later chapters.

Language learning as a social constructive process

Emerging from the work of Russian psychologist Lev Vygotsky (1896–1934) was the link between language learning and cognitive development which provided clear directions to educators that learners are assisted by the scaffolding provided by more expert users. Thinking about this a little more enables us to clearly see how a pedagogical model can emerge from Vygotsky's thinking – the idea that a task which is too difficult for a child to master alone can be learned with guidance from someone who can already do this task suggests a potent model for classroom learning. Vygotsky labelled this as the zone of proximal development (sometimes known simply as ZPD) – a novice learner begins the task and may become puzzled or confused, then the more expert other can assist by demonstrating the next level of the task. Often it is essential that the novice and the expert mediate this interaction with dialogue or talking. This idea further ascribed importance to the language learner's interlocutor who needed to recognize that the language addressed to young children needed to be focused, and delivered into the zone of proximal development.

Primary language education across the world has become aware of Vygotsky's influential ideas, and practice associated with scaffolding, more expert others and a clear focus on the language addressed to young children by teachers is apparent in the Primary National Strategy in England.

Emerging areas of language acquisition research

Currently there is again a focus on studies into language acquisition – both first language and additional language acquisition. The current research activity centres on the ability of researchers as never before to see inside the brain; using large man–machine interface (MMI) machines researchers can look at brain functioning while language learners are learning and using language. The studies started originally looking at medical patients who had lost the ability to use language and this then moved to looking at language learning. Researchers, teachers and curriculum designers need to follow these studies closely over the next few years and monitor the pedagogical implications, especially in relation to those children learning English as an additional language (EAL) in schools and those children whose language acquisition and use may not conform to expected progression rates.

English language as system

Every language has a system or a way that it functions – the identification and outlining of this system occurs sometimes after the language system is in everyday use. There are many languages used by humans, and some researchers even suggest that there are languages used by other species. The most famous of these, often described, is the way that bees communicate with each other through a series of dances which signal to the others where the best sources of honey are. This *language* is characterized by a system just as human languages have an elaborately documented system.

It is difficult to give an exact figure of the number of languages that exist in the world, because it is not always easy to define what a language is. It is usually estimated that the number of languages in the world varies between 3,000 and 8,000. The top five languages are Mandarin, Hindi/Urdu, Spanish, English and Arabic, although this is often disputed. Millions of speakers grow up and, without close tuition or instruction, manage to speak their mother tongue by the time that they are 5 years old. Languages are dynamic and can change and adapt to circumstances – already in learning to be a teacher you will have begun to add some new words or vocabulary to your language and within a few years your language will have adapted and changed to help you become a teacher.

Each of these 3,000 to 8,000 language systems is complex and has taken scholars many years to describe. The ways to describe languages are sometimes called a grammar.

As soon as we talk about grammar some of you might think 'Oh no! This is a topic that I know nothing about'. David Crystal (2006) gives us a reason why the word 'grammar' might make you nervous. He talks about the history of teaching grammar in Britain in a way that helps us think about grammar in schools and gives us an overview of how the teaching of grammar took place in schools over the past 50 years. Before the 1960s traditional grammar was taught in primary schools and this involved a close focus on correct usage and the analysis of sentences; some of this pedagogy was derived directly from the study of Latin grammar.

After the 1960s and before the 1990s, and connected with what is sometimes known as progressive pedagogy, grammar was not taught as a discrete subject but treated more as an investigation into language use, with minimal use of grammatical terms, such as nouns and verbs. From the mid-1990s, when the National Literacy Strategy become more central to the teaching of English literacy in schools, a renewed interest in teaching about language emerged often with a focus on the difference between written and spoken English.

Traditional grammar

This grammar taught people to analyse a sentence by making sense of the word classes and divisions within the sentence; sometimes sentences were divided into subject and predicate – with the predicate being divided into verb and object. This continued until all the features of the sentence had been identified. Sometimes this analysis or parsing is considered essential – like a doctor needs to know about anatomy to identify parts of the human body. However, if we focus too much on the detail of the language we can often lose focus on the use of language for communication. This leads us to the next type of grammar.

Descriptive grammar

The most important understanding about descriptive grammar is that it does not tell you how to speak or write – it describes how people use language. Analysts collected samples of language and attempted to describe the regular structures of the language as it was used, not according to a view of how it should be used. It works with a system of word classes, inflectional endings for tense and number, and a relatively short number of sentence structures. Descriptive linguists say that the English language system is characterized by three levels: (1) the grapho-phonic system, (2) the semantic system, and (3) the syntactic system.

Generative grammar

This manner of talking about language had its roots in the work of Chomsky (1957), who described language acquisition in relation to two levels – deep structure and surface structure. Developing from this to a notion that language learners were born with a knowledge of language as system regardless of the language that they were learning was known as universal grammar (Chomsky, 1965). Universal grammar (UG) is a theory of linguistics which suggests that there is a universal grammar that is shared by all languages, thought to be innate to humans. It attempts to explain language acquisition in general, not describe specific languages.

Universal grammar proposes a set of rules intended to explain language acquisition in child development: that all humans are born with a deep universal grammar which is shared by all languages, and that learners then pick up the surface features of language.

Systemic functional grammar

Michael Halliday (1987) in his work looking at language acquisition in the early years suggested that language acquisition is simply a series of choices that the learner makes. Each time you compose in oral or written language you make a series of choices about participants, processes or time markers.

Halliday's (1985) impressive book titled *An introduction to Functional Grammar* began to collect together his growing system or way of describing the English language. This has been an influential movement in education and has most notably contributed to the teaching of story-writing in primary schools.

So far, we have talked only about the English language and, when talking about language acquisition, have referred primarily to English as a mother tongue. It all becomes much more complex when we begin to talk about other languages and the ways linguists have developed to talk about them. If you learnt a foreign language in high school or primary school, or even when you have been abroad, then you will know that sometimes along the way you find out more about your first language or mother tongue.

This topic has so interested researchers in the past 100 years or so that there has been very focused enquiry into second language acquisition (SLA) and this in turn has assisted English language scholars in devising ways of describing language which assists those learning English as a second language (ESL) or those learning English as an additional language (EAL) or even those learning it as a foreign language (EFL). These three acronyms can often be troublesome for those who think about teaching English – so here is an easy way to think about it:

Task box

Using the definitions below, your task is to discuss with a friend and think about people you know or have met who are learning/have learnt EAL, ESL or EFL.

EAL – those learners who are learning English as an additional language, and perhaps already know one or two others (even if these are spoken only in very specific contexts). The use of this language would be in everyday life and possibly for education or working. The context in which the language is being learnt is an English-speaking community, for example, the UK, the USA or Australia.

ESL – those learners who are learning English to be able to speak it in their everyday life at work and at school. This is predominately used when we know that this is the first other language that the speaker is learning. Because the language is being used in everyday life, it is expected that the context that the language is being learnt in is an English-speaking community. For example, the UK, the USA, Canada or Australia.

EFL – this is where the language is being learnt in a language context where not many other people speak English. Thus the language is seen as a foreign language within that language community. An example is learning English in China with a view to moving to the UK to study at university.

The whole area of SLA research has generated many different ways of describing the English language, and these are used in the vast array of teaching and learning materials that have been developed for EAL, ESL and EFL learners.

The teaching of English grammar in primary schools in England

The National Literacy Strategy (NLS) and the Primary National Strategy – Literacy have chosen to describe language using the following three levels: word level, sentence level and text level. This model of looking at language appears to be derived from descriptive grammar (which describes how people use language) and the writers of the National Literacy Strategy: *Grammar for Writing* reference Professor Richard Hudson whose work is clearly from the broader field of descriptive linguistics. Here is an example of a typical list of grammatical items from the field of descriptive linguistics:

Adjectives	Verb tenses	Apostrophes	Audience
Capitalization	Adverbs	Complex	Compound
Conditionals	Commas	sentences	sentences
Exclamation	Conjunctions	Connectives	Direct speech
marks	Formal	Full stops	Grammatical
Imperative	language	Note-taking	agreement
Paragraphing	Negatives	Pluralization	Nouns
Presentation	Passive	Punctuation	Prepositions
Question	Pronouns	Reported speech	Purpose
marks	Questions	Subordinate	Simple sentences
Speech marks	Standard English	clauses	Verbs

English language as a vehicle for learning

The links between language and learning are well established and in the UK were very formally promoted in the Bullock Report (DES, 1975) which clearly states: 'It is the role that language plays in *generating* knowledge and *producing new forms* of behaviour that typifies human existence and distinguishes it from that of all other creatures' (DES, 1975: 47: original emphases). One of the consequences of the Bullock Report internationally was a focus on language as a vehicle for learning. This was also in tune with other research findings of the time, most notably Bruner (1975) who proposes that language and thought are central to language as a vehicle for learning and describing *linguistic competence, communicative competence* and *analytical competence* as being the key skills that the language learner requires to both access the curriculum and to demonstrate knowledge and understanding.

A further key theorist of the importance of the links between language and learning was James Britton. James Britton has been said to be the chief architect of a theory of language and learning which has influenced the thinking and practice of several generations of teachers, both in the UK and in the USA, Canada and Australia. Corson (1988: 14) concludes the first chapter of his well-known book *Oral Language across the Curriculum* with the statement: 'A good deal of schooling is devoted to "language on display"; the chief objective of the school is to encourage mastery of the language of the culture.'

The next chapter picks up this issue and moves forward with the discussion about the role of language in learning.

LEARNING AND TEACHING LITERACY

CHAPTER 2

ORAL LANGUAGE

ROBYN COX

'I wish my class wasn't so talkative and they would just settle down to work.' When I was a young teacher, I thought that a silent class automatically meant a class that is working and that I would be admired by my colleagues and the head teacher for 'building this purposeful learning context'. I now know that perhaps this was not the case. I am also surprised that I really believed this as I know when I want to work, think and solve problems that I need to talk and talk a lot.

When did the acceptance of talk in the learning context become widespread? And, more importantly, is it common and what do the curriculum guidelines about the place of talk in learning say? The following chapter takes a very strong stance on the centrality of talk in learning, and rationalizes this by referring to the work of two researchers who have investigated exploratory talk and the dialogic classroom.

This chapter includes:

- mother-tongue child oral language development
- the emergence of the idea of exploratory talk and a focus on the research methodology associated with the development of this pedagogical practice
- Alexander's dialogic classroom
- planning for and ensuring that talk is central to learning in the primary English classroom
- questioning in the primary English classroom.

Talk is a fundamental part of a child's development and it is usually something that parents and caregivers are the most unconcerned about when bringing up their child. The acquisition and development of mother-tongue oral language in children is a substantial topic in the child psychology, child development and, therefore, education literature, and there is a significant and rich research literature in the field. It is always interesting to note that a number of the key researchers of language discussed in the previous chapter began their research careers looking at children's language development and then went on to expound important linguistic theories.

This chapter looks briefly at the developmental aspects of children's language; it is commonly thought that mother-tongue development is mostly over by 5 years of age. The chapter then looks closely at talk in the primary classroom, in particular from a sociocultural perspective drawing mainly on the work of Mercer (2000) and Alexander (2008). The research findings promote the idea that a classroom where genuine dialogue takes place is the optimal environment for learning to take place.

The chapter then moves to explore four different contexts for classroom dialogue originally identified by Stables (2003), and how teachers need to make sure that these contexts are available for learners in their primary English classrooms. In closing, the chapter explores the newly underscored centrality of listening and speaking in the new primary curriculum (Rose, 2009).

The development of child oral language

There are many descriptions of developmental characteristics of child language, and these can often be very useful to look at for those beginning to work with children. However, we need to remember that some

Table 2.1 Typical language growth

0–6 months	Child turns head to listen to sounds. Makes all possible language sounds as play
6 months–1 year	Responds to own name, voices of others and environmental sounds. Might use single group of sounds as a word (dada and so on)
1–2 years	Uses 1 or 2 word phrases (for example, there bird). Follows simple spoken directions. 300–500 word vocabulary
2–3 years	Child develops own rule systems. Uses simple and compound sentences. Begins to use plurals, pronouns and prepositions. 800–1000 word vocabulary
3–4 years	Uses verb past tense. Overgeneralizes tenses and plurals (for example, I goed to McDonald's). Understands number concepts and includes adjectives and adverbs in more complex sentences. Begins to scribble, draw and copy writing. 1,000–2,000 word vocabulary
4–5 years	Tells stories about recent events. Follows a sequence of directions. Language use is becoming more abstract. Begins to recognize some letters and words. 3,000 to 5,000 word vocabulary

children develop language more quickly than others. I have included Table 2.1 because it gives an indication of a general pattern.

It is more important to realize that many, many children's language development does not follow this typical pathway, rather than focusing on the typical progression. Children with language delays or difficulties first need their language accepted as it is – the meaning and effort made to communicate must be rewarded rather than constantly corrected. A useful way of thinking of this, which comes from professional practice of English as an additional language (EAL) teachers, is the idea of 'recasting'; when a child uses language which we might not consider correct then it is always a good idea to 'recast' this language correctly in your response. The constructed dialogue below demonstrates this:

Child: Tomorrow day I go to my cousins
Teacher: Oh that is interesting, tomorrow you are going to visit your cousins. What will you do there?

You can see how the teacher rewards the attempt at communication by responding positively, recasting the usage errors into the correct form, and then further extending the communication by asking a question.

Dialect differences also need similar support in the classroom. This is an area which often concerns young teachers and you should become aware of the practice in relation to this in the school community. An English dialect is a variation of English that is characteristic of a region or social group.

Task box

Think of some word uses or pronunciation, or even sentence structure, that you use at home or with your peers or at university, which is not used in another of your language interaction groups. What is this an example of: vocabulary, grammar, pronunciation, style or perhaps intonation? List them and check your list with friends or colleagues. Are there any differences? Do you have any ideas why these differences occur? How would you feel if someone told you it was incorrect or suggested that you change the way you speak?

The Bullock Report (DES, 1975) left readers with the strong impression that, 'No child should leave their language at the classroom door'. Reflect on this in relation to dialect difference.

English as an additional language learners also need special support during their acquisition of the oral aspects of a second language; often this is a language system which has a vastly different sound system to the one that they have been listening to since they were born. The learners need to begin to notice the new sounds and then try them out. This is a daunting task, as I am sure you have all experienced when visiting a foreign country and having to cope. You need to listen to the language addressed to you, formulate a response cognitively and then put some words together in the foreign language to respond. This can be an overwhelming task – please remember this every time you are with a child who is doing just what you might have to do while abroad on holidays.

Sociocultural research and 'exploratory talk'

The idea of the classroom as a social learning space owes its legacy to the work of Vygotsky (1962, 1978) and his work showed that learning occurred mainly through linguistic interaction, and the dialogue with the more learned other being central to the process and thus establishing the idea of the zone of proximal development (ZPD). This view firmly established that dialogue and talk can supply 'scaffolding' where teachers can generate activities through which students can move their understanding of taught content further forward. Bruner (1966) was influenced by some of Vygotsky's work and studied the language of young children extensively about how one person can become very closely associated with another's learning. Bruner (1978: 19) writes: '[Scaffolding] refers to the steps taken to reduce the degrees of freedom in carrying out some task so that the child can concentrate on the difficult skills she is in the process of acquiring.'

Research from a sociocultural perspective has offered an alternative view to Piaget's cognitive developmental sequence, which emphasized individual action rather than interaction (for example, Piaget, 1970). This has led to questions about pedagogical models and curriculum structures that are focused on individual achievement rather than group processes. There is no doubt that teaching involves communication: this communication can be transactional – 'moving the lesson along'; informational – 'to deliver information or skills'; or social exploration – 'to get learners working communicatively in groups'. Stables (2003) draws our attention to the conflict that exists between transmission (as in transactional and informational) and empowerment in the classroom (as in social exploration). How can the teacher provide a context where this can take place? Perhaps the current National Curriculum regulations (DFEE and QCA, 2000) tends to provide levels of attainment that do not focus on effective classroom dialogue.

It has been suggested since the time when teachers, researchers and curriculum developers paid more close attention to Vygotskian perspectives on teaching and learning, that the value of authentic talk both between teacher and students and between students became apparent. This led to the identification of 'exploratory talk' by Mercer et al. (1999). Broadly, it is talk 'in which partners engage critically but constructively with each other's ideas. Statements and suggestions are sought and offered for joint consideration. These may be challenged and counter-challenged, but challenges are justified and alternative hypothesis are offered' (Mercer et al., 1999: 97).

The study by Mercer et al. (1999) set out to explore if a classroom where talk and dialogue was central was able to increase children's use of language for reasoning and collaborative activity. This study found that:

- using 'exploratory talk' helps children to work more effectively on problem-solving tasks
- using a specially designed programme of teacher-led and group-based activities, teachers can increase the amount of 'exploratory talk' used by children working together in the classroom
- children who have been taught to use more 'exploratory talk' make greater gains in individual scores on a test of reasoning than do children who have not had such teaching (Mercer et al., 1999: 108)

Clearly, exploratory talk should be incorporated into lessons, and most particularly English lessons, and the ground rules for this kind of talk can be taught. A number of other researchers and theorists have also advocated this approach, proposing that if the 'ground rules' of educational language practices were more carefully explicated, justified and 'scaffolded' by teachers, this would improve the quality of whole-class, group-based and individualized activities in the primary classroom (Mercer et al., 1999).

What, then, might these 'ground rules' be? As a primary initial teacher education student you will want to provide a context where 'exploratory talk' is possible in your classroom.

One set of rules put forward by Edwards and Westgate (1997: 115) illustrates some possible joint goals for communicating as part of a group:

To be a good member of a group:

1   Listen to what others say.
2   Wait for a pause before you speak – think about your words.
3   When taking turns, watch others and be ready when your turn comes round.
4   Be polite. Say what you think with respect for others.
5   Share things that you all need for the task and look after group equipment.

I am not sure that these are the ground rules that Mercer et al. were referring to; this seems like a set of polite behaviours that we would expect to be operating in any situation where people come together to communicate. Let us see if we can get closer to a version of classroom 'ground rules' of educational language practice that might develop higher-level reasoning skills.

The following list (from Mercer, 1995) provides a set of conditions more than 'rules' but I think assists us in our quest to develop activities which can help our primary learners to use 'exploratory talk':

1   Partners must have to talk to do the task, so their conversation is not merely an incidental accompaniment.
2   The activity should be designed to encourage co-operation, not competition, between partners.
3   Participants must have a good shared understanding of the point and purpose of the activity.
4   The 'ground rules' for the activity should encourage a free exchange of relevant ideas and the active participation of all involved. (Mercer, 1995: 98)

Task box

When you are next in a primary classroom, or even reflect on a classroom you have recently been in, think of a small-group activity that you have seen take place and complete the following grid:

Add a ✓ or X

Activity	Did the task **require** the children to talk to do the task?	Did the activity **encourage co-operation** or competition?	Did the pupils have a **shared understanding** of the purpose of the task?	Did the activity encourage a free exchange of **relevant** ideas?

How easy was it to complete this grid? Could you remember the details of the activity well enough, or perhaps you did not get enough information from just observing the lesson? Can you think of a small-group activity that you have designed and taught lately – did it achieve Mercer's (1995) conditions?

The 'dialogic classroom'

Robin Alexander (2001) has demonstrated how, by reference to a comprehensive international comparative study, national and regional contexts impact on classroom dialogue. For example, he points out that there is much greater emphasis on informal teacher talk in the UK and the USA than in India, France or Russia.

Wolfe and Alexander (2008: 3) suggest that a 'radical shift in thinking is not what is required but a movement towards change by increasing awareness of possibilities'. Alexander identifies the two different forms of talk – discussion and dialogue – as having strong potential for cognitive development. What is meant by dialogic interactions? A good definition is that supplied by Alexander himself: 'Children are exposed to alternative perspectives and required to engage with another person's point of view in ways that challenge and deepen their own conceptual understandings' (Alexander, 2008: 4)

The important contribution of Alexander's work has been the importance that he has ascribed to the difference between 'interactive' teaching understood by teachers, and the more focused idea of 'logic and rational argument' (Alexander, 2008: 4). Interactive teaching is that which by definition exists and has existed in primary classrooms in England for many years. It might be suggested that both Mercer's 'exploratory talk' and Alexander's 'dialogic teaching' are a very well articulated call for teachers to focus much more on bringing children to great cognitive understandings via very well designed classroom tasks.

Planning classroom contexts for the educational use of talk

If we accept that both 'exploratory talk' and the 'dialogic classroom' are what you as an emerging primary teacher would want to encourage to support our teaching and the pupil's learning then let us think a little more closely about how these contexts might be organized.

Looking at Stables's (2003) research into classroom dialogue allows us a systematic way of thinking about the opportunities for classroom talk.

Context 1: teacher–student/teacher–class dialogue

Much of this type of dialogue is characterized by the traditional teacher-led IRE (initiation–response–evaluation). Stables (2003) calls this asymmetrical because the power is held by the teacher and none is invested with the learner. An example of this is illustrated by Mercer's work:

Teacher:	How many parts are left here?
First pupil:	Seven parts.
Teacher:	Answer fully. How many parts are there?
First pupil:	There are ... there are seven parts.
Teacher:	How many parts are left? Sit down my boy. You have tried. Yes?
Second pupil:	We are left with seven parts.
Teacher:	Good boy. We are left with seven parts. (Mercer, 1995: 28)

The existence, dominance and monopoly of IRE in classrooms across time and geography is in no doubt, and it must be remembered that teachers use this in a balanced and skilful way in many lessons a lot of the time.

Context 2: between-student dialogue

Often in response to the recognition of the dominance of IRE, teachers have increased collaborative talk in their primary classrooms. A good example of this, strongly promoted by the National Curriculum (DFEE and QCA, 2000), is *talking partners.* There is strong evidence (Mercer et al., 1999), and further emerging research evidence, that there are good educational gains being made from these types of activities. A focus on the centrality of talk in the primary classroom and developing a classroom culture of dialogue will result in a more symmetrical notion of classroom interaction where power is distributed more evenly. What is seen to be an important element of this symmetrical notion of classroom interaction is that the negotiation of the task can at times be more important for learning than the successful completion of the task. This, of course, needs to be balanced against current National Curriculum regulations (DFEE and QCA, 2000) which tend to provide levels of attainment based on completed tasks and not necessarily on effective classroom dialogue.

Context 3: within-student dialogue – student and text

Some of Vygotsky's (1928) original ideas were about the learner's 'inner speech', which suggests that the learner often has to engage with a 'text' or some type of language-based activity that is physically separate from the teacher. However, this 'inner speech' is something that teachers do not often think about or pay attention to – is that because we cannot hear it?

We know very little about the quality of this speech or dialogue – perhaps if the pupils are quiet while they are reading the book, or focused while listening to the teacher read and we judge the 'atmosphere' as being focused or settled, then this within-student dialogue will be working well. A series of questions surface here: are all the pupils involved in the same level of 'inner speech' about the text? Is there any way in which we can ascertain this? Are comprehension questions at the end of a reading passage any gauge of the quality of this 'inner speech', similarly, book reviews or book talks?

Context 4: within-student dialogue – reflection and problem solving

This aspect of the within-student dialogue is less clear to teachers and those who write and disseminate the curriculum. However, the *Independent Review of the Primary Curriculum* (Rose Review) (Rose, 2009) has foregrounded the need for teachers and schools to provide contexts where problem-solving and reflection rather than content are at the centre of the curriculum.

Questioning

Primary classrooms are often dominated by teachers' questions and there are even suggestions that since the arrival of the National Literacy Strategy there has been an increase in the time that teachers spend asking questions and waiting for answers. A recent meta-analysis of research in teacher interaction in primary schools suggests that:

> Teaching in today's primary schools at Key Stage 2 is very much a matter of teachers talking and children listening … When questions are asked of children, these questions require them either to recall facts or to solve a problem for which their teachers expect a correct answer. Open or speculative or challenging questions, where children are required to offer more than one answer are still comparatively rare. (Galton et al., 1999: 33)

What are the main types of questions that teachers might ask and what are open, speculative or challenging questions? It has been suggested that the key difference between open and closed questions lies in the opportunities each type of question creates for classroom interaction. For example, open questions typically have multiple answers which are open to discussion and negotiation, whereas closed questions are usually understood to have a 'correct factual' answer.

Myhill and Dunkin (2002) provide this useful description of questions

- *Factual questions*: questions requiring a predetermined answer.
- *Speculative questions*: questions inviting a response with no predetermined answer. The answers to these questions were often opinions, hypotheses, imaginings or ideas.
- *Procedural questions*: questions relating to the organization and management of the lesson.
- *Process questions*: questions inviting children to articulate their understanding of learning processes or explain their thinking.

Task box

Reflect on your classroom experience and write below some questions which could be examples of each of these types of questions:

Open question:
Closed question:
Factual question:
Speculative question:
Procedural question:
Process question:

You should also refer to Medwell's Chapter 8, in this volume, where she discusses questions that might be used to probe how children think as they read and write.

A commentary from the United Kingdom Literacy Association (UKLA, 2010) contains what this professional association of primary English teachers suggests is an Agenda for Action for the twenty-first century. It places at the top of the list 'a more coherent approach to listening and talking as central to the curriculum'. The UKLA then draws attention to the programme, Every Child a Talker.

Every Child a Talker is a recent £40 million government programme to provide training and support to those working with young children in early years language development. The programme aims to improve practitioners' knowledge and understanding, enable them to support the development of children's speaking and listening skills, and identify at an early age any children with problems.

For teachers, the importance of talk in the classroom cannot be overestimated. However, the key to thinking about talk in the classroom is to foreground that classroom talk that is genuine and not always in response to teacher questions and teacher-led discourse.

Concluding comments

The next chapter, 'Reading' by Andrew Lambirth, presents a very rich account of the field of research and theory in the teaching of reading. The best way to teach young children to read is one of the most contested areas in the teaching of reading and if you read Chapter 3 immediately after Chapter 2 you will see how oral language provides a backdrop for the development of reading.

READING

ANDREW LAMBIRTH

An informal dialogue between an experienced teacher educator (TE) and a long-term head teacher and lead mentor (HT) in a school:

HT: Hi, I had another student the other day telling me that she does not really know how to teach young readers to read as she has not covered it in university, is that so?

TE: We have had this conversation before over the years haven't we? Student teachers invariably say that they are unsure how to teach reading, even though we cover the topic very early on in their course and visit it via a spiral curriculum model over the years before they graduate. I am not sure why this is so. I do often wonder about it – perhaps it is because the teaching of reading often becomes a political football – and young teachers are nervous about confirming their choice of methodological approaches …

HT: I think you are right – even at the moment the Simple View of Reading is contested by theorists and practitioners as not being so simple after all …

> *TE:* I think what student teachers need is a very clear and concise overview of the methodological choices for the teaching of reading, together with something that links this theory to what they might see in school.
>
> *HT:* Yes, now where could we get that ...
>
> Luckily we have the very chapter in this book that fulfils just this ... written by Professor Andrew Lambirth from Greenwich University.

This chapter includes:

- psycholinguistic approaches to the teaching of reading
- cognitive-psychological approaches to the teaching of reading
- phonics – syntactic and analytic
- the Simple View of Reading
- sociocultural approaches to the teaching of reading.

It is my view that if you want to be an outstanding teacher of reading, you need to take a professional approach. A professional reading teacher is enthusiastic and passionate about her field of practice, determined to do her best to ensure the educational well-being of the children in her charge. She will draw on the methods and procedures based on a body of theoretical knowledge and research, generated in universities and other research institutions or associations (Carr and Kemmis, 1997). Armed with this knowledge and love of her job, as one of a body of practitioners in a school, she will take autonomous decisions, informed by professional knowledge, about teaching reading to the individuals in her class. Professionals operate in this way. Drawing on this perspective, I intend to examine what one must know and what one can do to encourage children to read, and to read purposefully and for pleasure.

In this chapter, I introduce three main approaches to the teaching of reading that you will need to know if you want to begin to consider the approaches you wish to adopt in your classroom in consultation with your professional teaching team. All three approaches – psycholinguist, cognitive-psychological and sociocultural – continue to be influential. I examine the complexity of a teacher's task in encouraging children to read. As a developing professional, you will need to read more about these methods and talk to your tutors, teachers and peers, and then make a professional decision about the methods for teaching you and your colleagues will adopt.

Reading and being human: psycholinguistic perspectives

Do you remember how you learned to read? Many students I ask cannot remember. They often report memories of specific reading schemes, or cosy bedtime books with parents, but they often fail to remember how it happened and exactly when. Could this be because learning to read and write is a natural process? Noam Chomsky (1965) is a famous linguist who suggested that all humans have an innate predisposition to learn a language. Normally, for example, no one needs to be taught to speak; indeed, we appear to pick it up by our exposure to language around us and our need to communicate with others for survival. If this is so, could learning to read be natural too in some way? Literacy researcher Kenneth Goodman is one of the most famous scholars and teachers of reading. He is most often associated with a psycholinguistic understanding of how we learn to read. His view is that what makes language both necessary and possible is the human brain's ability to think symbolically (Goodman, 1996). Language is a tool that enables us to create complex systems that can represent even the most subtle experiences, concepts and ideas. For Goodman, it is a mistake to consider that written language learning is fundamentally different from learning oral language.

Task box

On a sheet of A3 paper draw your 'reading road'. It will start from one side of the paper and wind its way to the other. On this road, record significant moments in your personal reading history. It might begin with your bedtime stories with your parents, or more negative memories of reading in school. It might go on to include memories of reading-scheme books and might continue further on with GCSE literature moments – good or bad. Share the road with a friend and compare your experiences.

We learn to use written language later on in life, but Goodman sees this learning as no less natural than learning oral language. Both develop from the need for humans to think and communicate symbolically as individuals in society. 'Written language is an extension of human language development that occurs when it's needed: when face-to-face and here-and-now language is no longer sufficient' (Goodman, 1996: 118).

For psycholinguists like Goodman, literacy learning does not begin when children enter school. Literacy is not just a name for a lesson, it is part of life. Children arrive having had rich and varied literacy experiences, and have already learned to make sense of print. Goodman contends that schools can make the mistake of believing that the reading and writing curriculum is an entirely new set of skills for children to learn. Linked to this, is the view that schooling often 'pedagogizes' (Street and Street, 1991) literacy to the extent that we all begin to consider literacy as being learned only in school. It follows that, instead, teachers need to build upon and support what children already understand about language, both spoken and written. This will include a celebration of all the home languages brought into the classroom. Supporting children's language learning this way enables them gradually to control and manipulate the traditional conventions of written language. Children use their play to imitate the activities of the adults around them and gradually grasp the conventions needed to be mature and accomplished manipulators of written texts. We have all seen children 'inventing' written language, writing cards and notes that are often indecipherable to us, but painstakingly constructed by the children, and rich in meaning.

As all language is always used for authentic purposes, psycholinguists believe that children need to learn in authentic, meaningful and real situations, as opposed to environments made for class instruction, skills practice or discrete language drills. Children will learn most of what they need by using complete texts in real communicative situations, surrounded by a print-rich environment, reflecting the multilingual nature of our society, and where reading becomes a necessity to facilitate engagement in activities with print that proffers pleasure and gratification. This is often called a 'whole language approach'. Teachers in 'print-rich' classrooms and other adults outside school model a literate world, enticing children to participate by reading children's literature, discussing it, encouraging them to try to read for themselves and providing a range of strategies that will assist them in reading written texts. Perhaps, when you were growing up, you were enticed into the wonderful world of children's literature by a parent or a sibling, through cosy bedtime stories over a cup of cocoa.

For psycholinguists who promote this approach, reading requires that children know that they must bring their already developing knowledge of the world and their understanding of oral and written texts to make meaning from the written word. This is sometimes called a 'top-down' approach – it starts with the knowledge in our heads and brings meaning down to the print on the page.

From his research and analysis of reading behaviour, Goodman (1967) maintained that readers draw on three cueing strategies together to bring meaning from the text: grapho-phonic, syntactic and semantic cues. Grapho-phonic cueing is the way readers are able to decode graphemes (letters) into sounds (phonemes) – blending the phonemes to sound out a word. I go into more detail about this strategy later. Syntactic cueing strategies involve the reader drawing on his knowledge of language structures – grammatical constructions. 'The reader using pattern markers such as function words and inflectional suffixes as cues recognises and predicts structures' (Goodman, 1973: 25–6). In others words, a child's implicit understanding of how language utterances are structured enables the child to 'predict' what the next word will be in a written text.

The third cue is semantic. To derive meaning from the written word the reader needs to input knowledge about the world and specifically the world within which the meanings of the texts revolve. Knowing about the world, for example, that grass can be green and sky can be blue, enables children to predict what the next word will be in a text that has a sunny day as a context. A book that depicts a walk in the park enables children to draw on their knowledge of parks and the general experience of parks, utilizing the language around this context. For this strategy to be encouraged, it is important that the books available to children reflect everyone's culture and experiences. Marie Clay (1985) described how teachers orientate children to books by encouraging a conversation with them over the pictures, drawing out the vocabulary and the children's knowledge of that world. Once again, the reader gives something to the text (top-down) as well as the text giving something to the reader (bottom-up). With the help of adults and other more experienced readers, children learn to orchestrate their knowledge (Bussis et al., 1985) about language and the world by drawing on all these cues together.

As you will be starting to recognize, reading can be perceived as something much more sophisticated than just providing children with the skills to decode a text – sounding out the letters. The psycholinguists do not view reading as a form of technology, a set of technical skills to be simply learned in school. Reading is part of the way humans are able to utilize language to make meaning.

The teacher's role, using a psycholinguist approach, is to teach children how to draw on this knowledge by the creation of a 'reading classroom'.

A psycholinguist approach will include some or all of these features

- Reading aloud times – children hear written language read well from good quality books.
- An enthusiastic teacher with a love of language, in all its forms, and who promotes reading and writing and speaking and listening for pleasure and gratification.
- A core of quality multicultural and bilingual books in the classroom promoted well in a comfortable and welcoming surrounding. These books will be 'real books' – not reading-scheme books, written with the sole purpose to teach children to decode print. They will be children's literature written by authors with the intention of challenging and entertaining.

(Continued)

(Continued)

- Independent reading times – children can choose and read books together.
- Print displayed within a context – labels, announcements, favourite book titles.
- Opportunities to demonstrate the links between letters and sounds in times when teachers share books with children and when they write with the children. A classroom packed with displays of letters that have been discussed in class; alphabet books that are shared with the class.
- Word games and word play – I Spy, hangman and computer word games.
- Children reading one-to-one with a teacher.
- Book publishing and book-making.

With all these activities, the process of reading is promoted as an enjoyable and meaningful pastime and one that comes naturally to humans, conceived as the symbolic species (Deacon, 1997). Teachers are active in creating the situations, providing the resources and observing the development of the children in their care. They do directly teach their children in various ways after they have carefully assessed the individuals' needs. Teachers also appreciate the need to create environments that cause purposeful literacy events to occur.

Is this the way you want to teach children to read? Alternatively, do you believe that children need a more 'systematic', skills-based and staged approach?

Task box

When you are next in a primary school, look for methods and strategies that owe their presence to the psycholinguists. Use the list above as a guide. Talk to the class teacher. Did he or she know that they are a psycholinguist in some of their approaches?

Cognitive-psychological approaches: readers learn in stages

As a developing professional in education you will need to consider whether or not you believe that all children learn best through instruction in a series of stages. There is some contrast between supporting this method and the perspectives of the psycholinguists discussed above. Yet, we need to be aware of trying to avoid setting up oversimplistic binaries of contesting theory in reading pedagogy. Reading is complex. However, currently, governments all over the Western world are demanding that teachers see learning as happening in a staged and instructed way. The UK's *Independent Review of the Teaching of Early Reading* (Rose, 2006), known as the 'Rose Review' makes a case for the systematic teaching of reading which places grapho-phonic cueing strategies as the first and most important reading strategy that children must be taught. The word 'taught' is important here – instruction by the teacher is privileged by the author of this report. This pedagogical position is manifested in the previous government's document *Letters and Sounds* (Primary National Strategy, 2007) which is a six-phase (stage) teaching programme for the teaching of phonics throughout the Foundation Stage and Key Stage 1. For the anonymous writers of this document, they see it as essential that all children need to be taken through the same stages of learning – whatever their literacy background. I want to present this approach to teaching reading as being a cognitive-psychological approach (CPA). As a professional, you need a thorough understanding of this perspective in order to take decisions about your classroom reading pedagogy. The Rose Review has been heavily criticized by academics and teachers (Goouch and Lambirth, 2007; Hynds, 2007; Wyse and Styles, 2007) and you must take your place in the debate.

Those who support a staged and instructed model of teaching reading (Chall, 1983; Ehri, 1987; Frith, 1985; Gough and Hillinger, 1980) take slightly different perspectives, but unlike the psycholinguists, the CPA proponents see qualitative differences between what beginner readers need and what more experienced readers do while reading. The psycholinguists see the processes of reading as being the same for both novice and expert, but recognize that there are differences in the control early readers have over the reading process. Cognitive-psychological approaches make word identification the most important aspect of reading (Morris et al., 1996). This approach is more important than syntactic or semantic cueing strategies (mentioned above) and must be taught as the first cueing strategy. According to this approach, it will lead to better comprehension and readers that are made proficient more efficiently and much faster. Indeed, in modern English primary schools one could argue the 'race is on' to reach the standards expected by government policy at the end of each key stage from the moment children enter school. In this environment, speed of learning is crucial and one can also argue that it is important that children learn to read quickly in order to cope with other areas of learning – yet, at what expense?

For CPAs words matter (Hall, 2003) and some CPA research (Perfetti and McCutchen, 1987; Stanovich, 1992) suggests that children need to pay more 'bottom-up' attention to reading than psycholinguists seem to propose (Smith, 1971). As we have seen, psycholinguists give a great deal of significance to context clues – semantic and syntactic cueing strategies. Cognitive-psychological approaches research makes claims that the visual features of a text are used exhaustively by readers to make meaning and that context clues are simply not enough. This approach also contends that reading is in no way natural and that children need explicit teaching to ensure they master the decoding process. It follows, that children can do this by being taught in a systematic and methodical way through explicit instructed sessions, beginning when children are very young with learning the correspondence between letters and sounds – phonics.

Advocates of phonics have currently 'won' the argument in terms of current worldwide educational policy. Yet, you will need to question this rejection of reading as a meaning-building process, which the psycholinguists advocate, and the accompanying pedagogy discussed above. You will also need to examine the source of this pedagogy in terms of learning theories. It is clearly a behaviourist approach, which has many critics. In my experience, many teachers and educationalists hold the passionate belief that the psycholinguistic approach is a wise approach. You also need to consider if this universal intervention, advocated by pro-phonics lobbyists, takes into consideration all children's needs, and that some may benefit from a very different form of teaching altogether, perhaps something much closer to a psycholinguist's pedagogical position.

Phonics – synthetic and analytic – and the Simple View of Reading

The *Independent Review of the Teaching of Early Reading*, mentioned above, reports that: '51. having considered a wide range of evidence, the review has concluded that the case for systematic phonic work is overwhelming and much strengthened by a synthetic approach' (Rose, 2006: 20). Synthetic phonics programmes for the teaching of reading are those that put an emphasis on teaching children to convert letters (graphemes) into sounds (phonemes) and then blend the sounds to form recognizable words. The phonemes associated with particular graphemes are each isolated, pronounced and blended together (synthesized) to read and write the word – for example, d/o/g.

Segmentation means hearing the individual phonemes within a word; for instance the word c/r/a/sh comprises four phonemes. In order to spell, a child must segment a word into its component phonemes and choose a letter or combination (for example, 'sh') to represent each phoneme.

Blending means merging phonemes together to pronounce a word. In order to read an unfamiliar word phonemically, a child must attribute a phoneme to each letter or letter combination in the word and then merge the phonemes together to pronounce the word.

> ⌐ **Task box** ⌐
>
> While in school, examine the resources teachers are using to teach phonics. Read the teachers' handbooks and talk to teachers and children about their views on phonics teaching. Observe discrete phonics teaching in the school. Talk to teachers about 'why' they have chosen to use the schemes and resources you have found. Do they know about the research that has informed their practice? What is it?

This is an alternative approach to *analytic phonics* which aims to introduce children to whole words before teaching them to analyse these into their component parts. This approach emphasizes larger sub-units of words – *onsets*, *rimes* – as well as phonemes (Wyse and Styles, 2007). Onset is the part of the syllable before the first vowel. Rime is the part of the syllable from the first vowel onwards, for example, s/un, d/og, f/all, th/ink and m/eat. Analytical phonics methods emphasize that many single-syllable words deviate from the phonetic ideal of using one letter to stand for one vowel. For example, the vowel sounds represented by the letter 'a' here: 'cat', 'car', 'call' and 'cake'. Children are shown that we know how to pronounce the 'a' by looking at the letters that follow it. For example, words ending in 'ar', like 'far' and 'tar' all have the same sound value for the letter 'a'.

The differences between analytic and synthetic phonics has also caused arguments. The National Literacy Strategy was introduced in 1998 by the New Labour government. It was described as non-statutory, but was arguably enforced by national inspectors and was a highly prescriptive approach to the teaching of literacy for primary school teachers. It introduced detailed objectives for literacy lessons and provided a strict format to taught sessions. Its accompanying document was *Progression in Phonics* (DfES, 1998) which mapped out the stages of phonics teaching that policy-makers felt children needed to experience. Those who advocated synthetic phonics (for example, Johnston and Watson, 2003) were highly scathing of the phonics approach that *Progression in Phonics* offered. Research completed in Clackmannanshire in Scotland that looked at the use of synthetic phonics began to be the hailed by some (Burkard, 1999) as 'the Holy Grail of the teaching of reading' and as an end to illiteracy. It contended that synthetic phonics teaching had better results on children's reading achievement than other methods. The Clackmannanshire work has been criticized for its poor research design and its bias towards synthetic phonics (Goswami, 2007). The media promoted the Clackmannanshire work (Johnston and Watson, 2005), and very soon the Rose Review was commissioned to examine synthetic phonics methods, and came out in favour of its use. The Rose Review's findings are highly contested (Goouch and Lambirth, 2007; Hynds, 2007; Wyse and Goswami 2008; Wyse and Styles, 2007). In Wyse and Goswami's (2008) analysis of the research into the efficacy of synthetic phonics approaches, they state, 'the Rose Report's conclusion that synthetic phonics should be adopted nationally in England is not supported by empirical research evidence' (p. 706). The Report has also been criticized for, among other things, political bias. As students of reading pedagogy, you need to be aware of the notion of a 'politics of reading' (Styles and Drummond, 1993) which is said to pervade the profession. Sadly, we do not have time to pursue this, explicitly, here. The critics of Rose have been very clear about how they see the report:

> The Rose Review is a cunningly worded, politically motivated, dogmatic and dictatorial document. It purports to be, as witness its title, an 'independent review' of the teaching of early reading, but it is not independent and it is not a review. It is very obviously biased towards one particular 'phonic' method known as synthetic phonics' – a method regarded as narrow and limited by most eminent authorities in the field. (Hynds, 2007: 271–2)

As I have already mentioned, The Rose Review's position is manifested in the latest government non-statutory advice on early reading *Letters and Sounds* (DfES, 2007b) which advocates a staged synthetic phonics approach. There are many other commercial synthetic phonics schemes currently in use in school earning great wealth for their authors.

A systematic approach to the teaching of phonics might include the following:

- Daily whole class direct teaching sessions that practise sounding and blending of phonemes from the Foundation Stage upwards – this may include the use of songs based upon the alphabet.
- A government or commercial programme of lessons and resources.
- These taught sessions will have a regular structure – warm-up exercise – 'quick fire practice' and revision of previous teaching, introduction of new sound/s, word-making with magnetic letters, letter formation and consolidation (Macnair et al., 2006).
- A fast pace to the sessions is often recommended.
- Fidelity to the phonics programme is also recommended (Johnston and Watson, 2007). There should be no cherry-picking from programme to programme. Arguably, proponents of phonics are looking for 'teacher-safe' approaches to phonics teaching. Universal measures for teaching children to read are taken as being the wisest way forward – local needs are to be largely disregarded.
- Regular assessment by tests – observation by the teacher is not considered rigorous enough.
- A phonics-programme produced reading scheme based on what the children are learning in the taught sessions is often recommended to supplement the teaching.

- Those phonics advocates who suggest a more 'mixed approach' that sees phonics as only being part of the teaching of literacy will also ensure that the classroom has a good stock of attractive books.
- Reading resources will also include phonics games on the computer and elsewhere.

The Simple View of Reading

After being a teacher and academic for the past 20 years, I have begun to recognize the transitory nature of government policy on the teaching of reading. Since the demise of earlier advice from the New Labour government (the National Literacy Strategy, Progression in Phonics), the latest incarnation that has come from the 'Sturm and Drang' of the reading debate is the Simple View of Reading. This initiative has its basis in the cognitive-psychological approach of the Rose Review and is an adaptation of a position on reading pedagogy originally advocated in the 1980s (Gough and Tunmer, 1986). It proposes that reading should be conceptualized as being simple. In order to read, one must decode and then comprehend. Teachers need to begin by teaching young children how to decode by drilling and skilling in phonics, then proceed to teach comprehension skills. Children begin by 'learning to read' and then move on to 'reading to learn' – simple! When planning, teachers must differentiate between the two main objectives of their teaching of reading – decoding (word recognition) and comprehension. In this way children will learn more efficiently. That may sound like common sense to a layperson, but a professional needs to be as sure as they can that this is the best way to teach all children. It is a blanket approach based around behaviourist learning theory and, arguably, does not take into account the individual backgrounds, experiences and needs of the children who are to be taught. Is 'instruction' of this kind the best way to learn to read or is reading much more of a cultural process?

Learning to read as a cultural process: a short introduction to sociocultural approaches

'Who, then, are the children who do not fare well in early reading? Some are children with genuine neurological disorders making learning to read quite difficult. But the majority are poor or come from minority groups whose members have faced a history of prejudice and oppression (Snow et al. 1998). ... Why should being poor or a member of a particular social group have anything whatsoever to do with learning to read in school?' (Gee, 2004: 7)

There has been plenty of research that concludes that learning to read and write is a cultural process (Lave and Wenger, 1991; Rogoff, 1990). This means that there are some things within a culture that are considered so important that a society ensures that everyone who needs to learns to do it (Gee, 2004). Boosting one's communicative repertoires to include the use of the printed word is vital for modern societies to function and prosper – reading and writing have a huge cultural significance. Some believe that making reading culturally significant to *all* in society is the challenge for teachers in schools.

James Gee (2004) takes a sociocultural perspective on learning to read. Like the CPA, he does not believe that learning to read is a natural process. Yet, unlike the CPA he does not believe that learning to read is best completed through instruction in the ways discussed above. Gee (2004) describes learning to read as a cultural process. One learns best when what is learned appears purposeful, meaningful, and relevant in a familiar context. Gee states:

> Children who learn to read successfully do so because, for them, learning to read is a cultural and not primarily an instructed process. Furthermore, this cultural process has long roots at home – roots which have grown strong and firm before the child has walked into school. Children who must learn reading primarily as an instructed process in school are at an acute disadvantage. (2004: 13)

Gee contends that many children are not given, what he calls, prototypes of academic language skills from home when they first come to school. He gives examples of these prototypes as 'children doing pretend reading of books, that sound like the child is reading a real book, or children reporting at dinnertime on their day in a fashion that sounds like a school report' (2004: 19). Some families encourage their children to use language in this way, while others do not, but it is this academic variety of language that is rewarded in schools. It is not because those families who do not encourage this form of language are in any way poor parents, but rather that it is simply not part of their culture and communicative repertoires to use language in this way. Literacy always occurs in a cultural context (Street, 1984) and just as cultures differ within societies, so do the forms of literacy practices operating therein. School literacy is also not neutral or 'autonomous' (Street, 1984), it too has an ideological and cultural source. As Gee contends, some children will recognize these practices while others will not. The challenge is to give this form of language use and print-orientated events – including reading – a meaningful context for all. Providing instruction is not enough (Snow et al., 1998).

Advocates of this position (Rogoff et al., 2001) define learning as 'changing participation in culturally valued activity' (Larson and Marsh, 2005: 109) and that learning is co-constructed with others in routine everyday activities and social practices. A school reading curriculum must therefore focus on the interests of the children, and schools and must value children's home language use. Teachers need to research how children use language at home, the forms of text they enjoy – television, gaming and so on, and build upon these experiences to introduce alternative language use including the culturally empowering academic forms. Offering instruction alone, which is for some an alien uses of language, can inhibit engagement in schoolwork and helps to explain consistent patterns of underachievement in certain groups of children.

From a sociocultural perspective, schools need to create communities of learners (Rogoff et al., 2001) where children are socialized at multiple levels and are encouraged to participate in multiple forms of social practice using a variety of language use, which includes reading, but not at the expense or debasement of other forms of literacy practices. This would mean constructing a reading curriculum which is rich, engaging and relevant to all, and that does not offer instruction at the expense of participation.

Teachers wanting to adopt this understanding in their reading teaching might do some of what I have listed below. The practical manifestation of this perspective would use much of the psycholinguists' suggestions above, but with some significant differences about how 'reading' is conceptualized.

Sociocultural approaches

- Conceptualize reading in a broader sense – include the image, film, television and video and computer game texts.
- Find out what the children enjoy doing at home – leisure pursuits etc and build them into school life.
- Find out from the children what they would like to read and bring these texts into the classroom.
- Introduce more texts from popular culture into the classroom.
- Expand your reading area to include ICT equipment that can play video and gaming texts – include magazines and comics and attractive posters from the world of popular cultural texts.
- Be interested in and open to children's home literacy practices.
- Teach school-based literacy practices within a meaningful context – use real texts that children will enjoy and with which they can relate – bring in texts from popular culture at these times.
- Allow participation and allow negotiation about what should be taught and when with the children.

Concluding comments

Reading is not simple at all. It is complex. It is now down to you as a member of our profession to read and discuss the issues with academics and teachers and then make decisions about how the children you teach need to learn to read.

If you could join in the conversation between the teacher educator and the head teacher at the beginning of the chapter what would you have said? Would you support what the students are saying? Alternatively, how would you explain what you understand about the teaching of reading?

CHAPTER 4

WRITING

LIZ CHAMBERLAIN

The teaching of writing in recent years has focused primarily on each pupil producing a piece of writing that is suitable for levelling using the outcomes statements from the Primary National Strategy in Literacy. This is so that each pupil can be given a standardized achievement test grade. This is an emaciated view of the teaching of writing in relation to the research and practice literature, and is a very sad view of the place of writing in current schooling. Of course, my view presented here would be contested by many other teacher educators – but as an introduction to this chapter it provides a provocative stance.

The next chapter provides the reader an overview of the theory and practice in the teaching of writing and most importantly provides the building blocks for the development of aspects of creative writing which will no doubt underpin new curriculum developments.

> **This chapter includes:**
>
> * writing as communication
> * the teaching of writing
> * models of writing
>
>   – the skills based
>   – the genre approach
>   – the process approach
>
> * teaching and inspiring writers
> * planning for writing
> * creative approaches to writing.

As trainee teachers it is important that you know how to support young writers in the classroom and how to engage children in purposeful writing activities. One of the features of high-quality literacy lessons is where teachers have good subject knowledge and a clear understanding of the individual needs of their pupils (Ofsted, 2009: 53). As a writing teacher (Bearne, 2002), you need to have considered some of the wider debates about writing. For example, you may already have very specific views about the nature of English as a subject (Ofsted, 2009: 19), or you may have a particular attitude towards writing. Your attitude may be influenced by your current experiences, which may well be focused on the writing and passing of assignments which while for some of you this may be an enjoyable experience, others may find it a necessary chore to reach a greater goal. It is your attitude and approach to writing that will motivate writers in your class, and therefore, as with reading, you need to make professional decisions about what writing will look like in your classroom.

Over the past 10 years writing standards have steadily improved. However, by 2006 they began to plateau with the common feature of Key Stage 2 Standard Assessment Tests (SATs) results being the major discrepancy between achievement in reading and writing; with results in reading outscoring those in writing by as much as 14 per cent for girls and up to 22 per cent for boys (see Table 4.1) (National Strategies/DCSF, 2008; Ofsted, 2005).

Table 4.1 National Curriculum Assessments for English at Key Stage 2 in England (2009, DCSF)

Achieving Level 4+	Total	Girls	Boys
English	80%	85%	75%
Reading	86%	89%	82%
Writing	67%	75%	60%

There is much debate and discussion as to some of the reasons for this. As you consider the above results, you may reflect on the fact that girls do better than boys in writing. While this may be true for some boys, what else might it tell us? Maybe it is the writing tasks that we are asking children to engage in that lead to such differences and what is needed is a closer examination of writing practices rather than viewing boys as deficit models of writers. This is supported by what we know about writing; that the theory of how children learn to write, and how they can be supported in order to become successful writers is under-researched (Kress, 1994: Myhill, 2001). Hall (2003) puts forward the notion that for children to enjoy reading, they must see what reading is for and what it can do for them, and therefore it seems pertinent to ask the same of writing.

Writing as communication

What is suggested in this chapter is that writing is hard; it involves having ideas, having something to say. It also involves drawing together a range of skills that all come together at the same time to produce a carefully crafted piece of work. However, writing is also bound up in personal identity, in that other people may make judgements about you as a person by how your writing reads and, in some cases, what it looks like. You may remember feeling anxious about what to include within your personal statement for your course and you were right to feel that way. When your statement was read, by someone unknown to you, your application was either placed on the 'accept' or 'reject' pile. The content of your writing, as well as your use of grammar, punctuation and style were all judged and this is why writing is very different from reading; with writing you are creating the text while in reading you are interpreting text created by others. Later in this chapter you will be asked to consider a memorable writing experience and whether you consider yourself to be a good writer. Before you think about that, consider a primary classroom during quiet reading time; are you able to notice the good readers or those who are pretending to read? What about pretending to be a good writer, is that possible?

Task box

Write down a list of all the writing that you have done this week.

- What was the purpose of the writing?
- Who was the writing for?
- What did the writing do?
- How was the writing set out?

The teaching of writing

In reviewing your responses to the previous task, you have probably realized that different types of writing need different approaches. For example, on your list you may have referred to notes of some kind, maybe a shopping list, and this would have been an aide-memoire written to remind you of the items you needed while shopping. It may have been written on a scrap piece of paper or on the back of an envelope, and you probably took little care over the handwriting or presentation. However, with a letter to your grand-parents, you may have considered the paper to write on, whether it was to be handwritten or typed and there may have been some deliberate deci-sions about the content, which may have focused on the types of news that you know is important to them. What is clear in both examples is that there was a different intention for each piece of writing and that this intention influenced how the writing was presented. These two examples may also be viewed as the more traditional forms of writing and your list may also have included writing that did not involve using a pen or pencil. Do you con-sider text messages, SMS messages, Facebook comments, emails, Tweets, comments or online news comments or blog updates as writing? With the increase in access to technology, children and young people are engaged in a range of electronic forms of writing out of school. There is some evidence to suggest that young people who have their own social networking page have more positive attitudes towards writing (Clark and Dugdale, 2009). What is important here is whether you consider these kinds of activities as *writing*, as this will influence the kind of writing activities that you plan for.

So the question that you may be beginning to ask is, what exactly is writing? Frank Smith (1982), in his book *Writing and the Writer*, proposed that writ-ing is a powerful form of language and that it is much more than the simple translation of speech into the written word. He suggested that writing could be viewed as art, as communication or as a record. While it could be argued that all writing is communication, what of writing as art? As an art form, writ-ing can be the product of creativity, which may go beyond an imaginative output such as a story or poem, and instead it is the engagement with the artistic process that is enjoyed. However, not all children will engage with writing in such a creative way but what is crucial is that children are able to see writing as a means of communication, which is relevant to them. The spoken word is fleeting and relies on a shared experience, as the speaker is encouraged by the listener who can support, extend or even just acknowl-edge what the speaker is saying. Writing, however, is deliberate, it is precise and organized and in the crafting of a text a permanent record is created.

It is this idea that writing is permanent that may make it difficult for young writers, especially those who find spelling or handwriting challenging. Over recent years the concepts of 'record' and 'evidence' have become confused. There has been an expectation that pupils are writing in every lesson and that the writing output is somehow viewed as tangible evidence of learning, rather than as a meaningful process of communication. Some of the writing activities that we ask children to do in school are more about providing evidence that teaching has occurred, rather than having a real reason for writing. As a visitor to a classroom I do not need to look at a child's writing to know what they are learning; I can ask them. Writing in books should be untidy and messy, which demonstrates that writing has been allowed time to develop and to be drafted and refined. The work on display should be celebratory, informing or entertaining the reader. When wondering why writing achievement lags behind reading, it is worth considering the type of writing activities that children are engaged in and the choices behind them. If low-attaining children are spending time copying down learning objectives, are they really engaged in the potential for writing as Frank Smith describes it?

As a new teacher, you need to consider carefully the types of activities that you will plan for. The young writers in your class need to understand the purpose of the writing and for whom they are writing. For example, if children are learning about persuasive texts consider the kinds of writing that has persuasion at its heart; a letter to the school council about an important school issue, an article or online comment for the local newspaper about the litter problem outside school. Writing needs to be meaningful for children and if you take time to consider what you are asking them to write, you will find that writing can be the powerful form of communication that Smith describes.

Frank Smith also suggested that in order to understand the complexities and challenges of writing, it helped to separate it into two specific areas, transcriptional skills and compositional skills. Composition skills are concerned with getting ideas, the grammar and selection of words, in essence, doing what authors do, and the transcriptional skills involve the physical effort of writing, the spelling, capitalization, punctuation, paragraphing and legibility of the writing (Smith, 1982: 20). You may also see these terms referred to as authorship or secretarial skills (Latham, 2002) and what is being suggested is that writers bring together ideas *about* a piece of writing – the compositional skills – and skills *for* the writing – the transcriptional skills. While it may be obvious that in order to write, you need to have something to write about and the skills to write it down, Smith went further and argued that in order to be a successful writer, the compositional and transcriptional skills should be taught separately and that transcriptional skills should always be last (Smith, 1982: 23).

What Smith is arguing is that if we attend to the ideas for our writing, our transcriptional skills may suffer and if we concentrate on the handwriting and punctuation, then the ideas can dry up. Consider the shopping list written in a rush on the back of an envelope; the meaning is clear to you but it may well be difficult for anyone else to read. However, this does not matter as the writing was only for you and you know the meaning each particular scribble conveys. This is similar to a very young child at the beginnings of writing, where she appears to be making marks that resemble no more than circles or lines but then asks you to read back their writing. 'As the child discovers that speaking (with which he is familiar) can be conveyed in print he must set himself the test of understanding many arbitrary conventions which we as adults accept so readily' (Clay, 1990a: 2). What this young writer has discovered is that language has a written symbol and a specific form and that 'the meaning of the symbols can be retrieved and communicated orally' (Browne, 1993: 3). However, what she has also discovered is that there are rules for writing and that the marks that convey a specific meaning cannot be translated by you, which is why you may find yourself responding to the question, 'What does this say?' with 'Why don't you tell me'.

Models of writing

In Chapters 1, 2 and 3, you were introduced to the social-constructivist approach and it is useful consider how this approach can be applied to writing. You may already feel that what has been presented in this chapter has been from a social-constructivist view and you would be right. Writing is a social process where context is everything, as has been previously illustrated by the examples of the shopping list and the letter to grandparents. What, and how, you write is wrapped up in why you need to write and therefore purpose must be at the heart of the writing process. Jerome Bruner, one of the most influential of the social constructivists, suggested that 'knowing is a process not a product' (1966: 72). Eve Bearne (2002: 6) extended this notion to writing and posed the question: 'Writing: noun or verb?' If writing is a process, or an act of doing, then, you need to allow children the time to work on their ideas, change their ideas, talk about their ideas and then, when they are filled up with these ideas, it is at this point that the recording of the writing can happen. Pie Corbett talks about teachers inspiring children in such a way that they are on the edge of their seats 'wondering what writing task will come their way' (2005: 6). If you see writing as a noun or an output, and you intend to plan for children to complete a piece of polished work in every lesson, you may wish to ask yourself whether this is something that you could do.

The next section introduces you to three different approaches to writing that over the past 20 years have influenced how writing is taught in primary classrooms. At the end you may wish to reflect on whether you feel that writing is a process (verb) or product (noun), as this will influence your own practice and approach to writing activities.

The skills-based approach to writing

As much as Smith argued that ideas need to come first and that transcriptional skills can be worked on later, there is also the argument that developing automaticity in handwriting, and in turn spelling, will free up the cognitive resources needed to generate the ideas needed for the composition (see Chapter 7)(Medwell and Wray, 2007; Stainthorp, 2002). This approach to writing has its basis in cognitive psychology, and this is where the theory and debate about writing differs from that of reading, as theorists attempt to use models to explain what happens when, or as, we write. The skills-based approach draws on a 'simple view of writing' suggested by Berninger et al. (2002) which, in its most basic form, is represented by a triangle with transcription skills and the executive functions of planning, reviewing and refining at the bottom, with text generation at the top. Berninger et al. (2002) put forward the notion that if children freed up the time spent on transcriptional skills, by improving and increasing, for example, their spelling skills, this in turn may improve compositional skills and therefore lead to successful writing. Their argument is that anxiety or worry about the correctness of spelling may mean that, for some children, this becomes the focus of the writing rather than the expression of ideas. This view is certainly supported by what we know children say about writing; in one survey children considered *spelling* to be the key feature to becoming a good writer, with composition skills being considered the least important (Wray, 1993).

What is important about this approach are the implications for the teaching of writing. As practitioners, we are more confident in teaching transcriptional skills; we can mention the handwriting, correct the spelling and reflect on the effort involved (Black and Wiliam, 1998). Compositional skills and ideas are harder to comment on or to teach, and while you may agree that children need skills first in order to be able to write, it should not be at the expense of giving time for capturing the ideas for writing.

The genre approach to writing

The National Literacy Strategy (NLS; 1998–2006) was developed in response to ongoing concerns about the attainment of children's writing and at its core was a genre approach to writing (Fisher, 2006: 194). The NLS specified the types of writing that children should be taught, with a focus on a broader diet of genres, which included writing in the different non-fiction genres of explanation, recount, persuasion, discussion, reports and instructional or procedural texts. The guidance at the time, in the form of *Grammar for Writing* also suggested that children be introduced to a range of fiction and poetry writing (DfEE, 2000). Effective teachers of literacy were clear about how they interpreted the guidance but ensured they planned for purposeful writing with meaningful cross-curricular links (Fox et al., 2001). For example, explanation texts were planned in at the same time as the science topic of the Earth and Space, thus ensuring the opportunity to practise the skills of an explanation genre but using the content of the science topic. However, what also happened was that teachers felt pressurized into teaching too many genres too quickly, and in ways that did not lead to quality writing and instead the focus became on children 'demonstrating linguistic competence and knowledge retention' (Cremin et al., 2006: 273).

While it is important that children have an awareness of different text types, it is also crucial that they know when and how to use them, and can therefore make choices about the most appropriate form for their writing. While the new Primary National Strategy (DfES, 2006b) illustrates how teachers can be flexible with their planning, the Ofsted report *English at the Crossroads* would suggest that there is still an overemphasis on the technical competence of writers, rather than on engagement with writing: 'Sometimes the teaching focused more on pupils' knowledge *about* writing rather than on developing their skills *in* writing' (Ofsted, 2009: 26). What we do know about writing is that in order to improve writing you need to be doing writing.

The process approach to writing

Donald Graves (1983) was the lead proponent of the process approach to writing, which placed the child and their interests at its heart. He suggested that children and teachers should work together to create and craft writing, rather than be driven by a tick-list of skills or knowledge, as highlighted by the genre-specific approach. The key to this process was the use of the Writer's Workshop, with children deciding the topic of the writing and with the teacher taking on the role of guide or supporter. You may well have seen Writer's Workshop in Key Stage 1 classrooms, with children starting the day writing on topics of their own choosing and then sharing their writing. Graves also stressed the importance of an environment for writing, with children being surrounded by quality literature and for writing to be celebrated by being published or displayed.

You may agree that all of the above sounds like good primary practice and certainly Graves's work was reflected in the 1988 National Curriculum which emphasized that the writing process should include planning, drafting, revising, proofreading and presentation (DfEE, 1989). Criticisms of the process approach to writing were focused on the idea that children were leading the learning, which frightened politicians of the day and it was these concerns that led to some of the thinking behind the NLS (1998).

However, what was overlooked in the process approach was the importance that Graves placed on teachers knowing about writing and how to support children as writers. 'The teaching of writing demands the control of two crafts, teaching and writing. They can neither be avoided or separated' (Graves, 1983: 5). This emphasis on the role of the teacher remains crucial, as is the need for good subject knowledge (Ofsted, 2009). Interestingly, current guidance for the teaching of writing and the model presented by the Primary National Strategy Framework for Literacy (DCSF, 2007) would suggest a more process approach to writing.

Task box

What has been your most memorable writing experience and why?
Do you consider yourself to be a good writer?

Teaching and inspiring writers

When reflecting on your memorable writing experience, you may have found that your key writing experiences were often connected to how people responded to your writing. A parent or teacher may have praised your writing, or it was displayed in a classroom or even published in a book or anthology. You may have written a heartfelt letter or email that had unforeseen consequences or the reaction may have been a negative one, with a piece of writing being returned with red pen highlighting the errors in your work. Whatever writing you chose, it is unlikely to have been that cloze procedure you struggled with in Year 4; the point being made is that for writing to be effective, there needs to be a connection to the writing – a reason for doing it.

Young children engage with role-play writing before they come to school and you will have seen children in pre-school making lists, mark-making, experimenting with different media and enjoying the exploration of this new way of communicating. As children move into Key Stage 1 their writing experiences become increasingly planned for or dictated by the teacher with fewer opportunities for children to experiment with writing in the way that very young children do.

For writing to be powerful and for young writers to see writing as relevant to them, it is clear that the writing tasks they engage with need to be meaningful, have a clear audience and most importantly a reason for being written (Graves, 1983). This is different to what children say about writing, as previous research has suggested that children see writing as a series of technical skills, an activity that produces an output that can be measured and judged according to the quality of the handwriting and appropriate use of punctuation (Wray, 1993). However, if writing is to be considered an art, or for children to be designers of their writing (Maun and Myhill, 2005; Sharples, 1999), then consideration needs to be given to the factors that will allow children to produce a carefully crafted piece of writing – purpose, readership, form and choice.

Beyond the practical considerations in planning writing, what is crucial is the extent to which you are aware of your role in supporting young writers. Eve Bearne once again: 'teachers must write in the presence of their classes. This is rather different from the earlier sense of a teacher being a writer whose experience might act as a reflective guide as well of a demonstrator of techniques' (Bearne, 2002: 30).

In the past when teachers said, 'Today, we're going to do some writing' what was meant is, 'Today, I'm going to tell you to do some writing and I'm going to mark it when it's completed'. If you remember what Donald Graves was suggesting in the 1980s, it was the notion that teachers and children were writing together and in doing so engaging with a shared understanding of the creative process, which for many of us, leads to an awareness of the challenges and discomfort that writing can bring. Recent research would suggest that those teachers who engage as writers in their own classrooms transform not only their teaching of writing but change their attitudes and approaches to the types of writing opportunities they plan for (Cremin, 2006).

What this means is that you need to write, you need to write for yourself, you need to write with the children, in front of them, on your own and you need to be demonstrating to them what writers do, but more importantly you need to call yourself a writer. What was your response to the question, 'Are you a good writer?'

Task box

Ask children what they think about writing. Knowing what the children in your class think about writing will enable you to have a shared understanding of what writing is. Use the following questions as a starting point for your own survey on children's writing:

1 Do you have a favourite piece of writing?
2 What is it that you like about this writing?
3 What do you think your teacher looks for when marking your writing?
4 Is there someone in your class who is a good writer?
5 What kinds of writing do you like doing at home?
6 Are you a good writer?

Planning for writing

Having considered the why and the how of teaching writing, you also need to think through the what – what writing activities will you plan for? You know that writing needs to be meaningful with a clear purpose and ultimately an audience for the writing. When planning for writing it is important to slow down the process and allow time for ideas to be captured, changed and refined. The recent guidance outlined in *Improving Writing with a Focus on Guided Writing* (DCSF, 2007) suggests a model of the writing process based on the work of Eve Bearne (2002: 31). The initial stages focus on the familiarization of the genre or text, where children learn about the features of the chosen genre. They do this by reading and exploring texts across a range of modes, including books and multimedia texts. The next step is the capturing of ideas and this is the crucial stage, as this is where the compositional elements for the writing are collected. By allowing for activities like drama, talk time, partner work and planning, children will be immersed in their ideas for writing before moving into the final stages of recording. What is crucial throughout the process is the role of talk; in particular talk *for* writing and talking *about* writing (Myhill and Jones, 2009). This is a relatively new area of research and a recent study, *From Talk to Text* (Fisher et al., 2006) began to explore the role of talk in supporting writers. You may also hear teachers talk about a project called *Talk for Writing* (DCSF, 2008b), which is based on a set of resources developed by Pie Corbett, with a view to teachers using the approach and adapting it within their own classrooms. Myhill and Jones (2009) also suggest that children should have the opportunity to use talk to reflect on their writing and that by talking about their choices they continue to develop and refine as writers.

Planning for writing: the bigger picture

The starting point for any well-crafted piece of work is what you, as a teacher, have planned for. As you get to grips with the whole curriculum, what you need to ask is, 'Where does writing fit in with this particular topic, and where are the meaningful links?'

Consider the following example in Figure 4.1 for a Year 3 class in the autumn term with a focus on the creation of visitor guides for the Ancient Egypt museum they have recently established in their classroom, using artefacts from home and the local museum service.

Teaching sequence	Activities	Strategies
Familiarization with genre/texts	Read information books and visit museum websites, discuss the layout and multi-modal elements of the texts	Shared reading, guided reading, own research, note-taking, audio-recording, discussion, evaluation
Capturing ideas	Visit a local museum, design a questionnaire for museum visitors and interview the curator. Watch television clips of the discovery of Tutankhamen's tomb and hot-seat different characters. Create information labels for artefacts, research facts on Ancient Egypt	Drama activities, hot-seating, interviewing, researching, discussion, story-mapping, partner planning
Teacher demonstration: Teacher scribing Supported writing	Create your own visitor guide – decide on the presentation – use teacher's writing as a model to support children through the process	Shared writing, guided writing, reading, evaluating
Independent writing	Decide on mode of writing: interactive, paper-based, audio-visual	Talk for writing, talk partners, peer evaluators, sharing the writing

Figure 4.1 Planning a unit of work using the teaching sequence for writing

This is a simplified example of how you can approach your planning but you will notice the importance of making links between reading, writing, and speaking and listening. Having completed this topic and made meaningful links between the history topic of Ancient Egypt and the genre of information texts, children will have been using their research skills in history to support their understanding of what it is that information texts do. If the next literacy unit of work is adventure stories, then make the link with the children's prior knowledge, in this case an understanding of Ancient Egypt, and you have found the setting for their stories. The children will have the historical knowledge to make their stories authentic, while your teaching points will be focused on the often complex genre of an *adventure* story.

Ensure that you have considered the bigger picture and planned for your class book or novel to be one whose theme is adventure. Children need to be exposed to quality texts, both fiction and non-fiction, so that they interact with, and read, good models of a range of texts, both print and electronic, which will support their own writing. Barrs and Cork (2001) refer to this as 'the reader in the writer' and maintain that children who know how texts work are more likely to be successful writers (Flynn and Stainthorp, 2006: 61). By reading to children a story genre that they are writing they can listen to and talk about the key elements of the story and you will also find that they begin to use the ideas they hear in the story within their own writing. By planning in this way, you are not overwhelming children with too many new pieces of information; instead you are layering up their learning by leading and supporting them through the writing process.

Task box

When planning a literacy unit of work, choose a text that will support children's understanding of a particular genre and ask yourself the following questions:

Purpose: Why am I planning this writing? Why am I asking children to do this writing?

Readership: Who is this writing for?

Function: What does this writing do: send a message, give information, tell a story?

Form: How will this writing be set out? What will this writing include?

Consider the amount of time that you are planning for:

Finding out about **texts**
Capturing **ideas**
Planning **ideas**
Talking about **ideas**
Writing **aloud**
Evaluating their **ideas** and **writing**

Creative approaches to writing

As you reflect on the above task, you may wonder where teachers find inspirational ideas for writing. One resource that schools use is Everybody Writes, a web-based project aimed at celebrating innovative approaches to writing, allowing schools to take a fresh look at the writing opportunities within their own school and how they can bring the essential creative element to their planning. Schools have taken the Everybody Writes approach and used it as a framework to support creativity in their own settings, while considering what writing means for their school by allowing children choice over their writing.

Letter writing for the whole school

One school hosted an Everybody Writes day with the aim of raising the profile of writing for children who may not see writing as necessarily relevant to their lives. On one day every child in the school was asked to choose an occupation that they wanted to do when they were older and to write to someone whom they admired to ask them how they used writing in their job. Teachers were amazed at the range of occupations and also found out things about their children that were new to them. One boy wrote to the editor of a fishing magazine who responded with an invitation to join a local angling club, while another child wrote to a paramedic who subsequently arranged to visit the school in an ambulance. Many children did write to famous footballers and television stars, but the letters that left the most impression were those from local people who did local jobs. The teachers realized that many of the children had never written a letter or addressed an envelope before and ensured that the whole school shared in the excitement as the letters were returned and read out in assembly. The purpose and audience for the writing was clear and the children and teachers were able to appreciate the power of writing as a means of communication. For some of those children there was a realization that writing goes beyond the school walls and that it can be relevant to their lives and futures. For the teachers they realized that the planning for writing does not have to be complicated; what is important are the preparation and the intention behind the writing.

Reflection

As you review your understanding of the writing process, how young writers develop and the importance of your role, you may agree that writing is hard. Writing is also messy and untidy, and sometimes it can be slow, but if you take the approach that children need to engage with writing in meaningful ways, then the choices you make as a teacher, will impact on how the children in your classes view writing. By ensuring that the writing in your class has an authentic audience and a clear purpose, children will see writing as going beyond the classroom and as relevant to them.

As well as your choices in planning, you need to consider your role as a writing teacher. It is crucial that children see you write in lessons beyond literacy, in mathematics, in history, in Golden Time, and by being a role model for writing you will be showing children that you value writing. Take time to plan your classroom; ensure that there is a writing corner or, if space is difficult, have a writing wall where you can write a comment of the day and let children respond. It is not difficult to showcase writing so that children know that your classroom is one where writing is supported, through interactive displays, and celebrated, through quality work highlighted on walls, in books and on the computer.

Consider your own subject knowledge, what do you know about a specific piece of writing, how will you know when a child's writing is good and how will you tell them? Ensure that you plan time each week to work with guided groups on their writing and let children in on the game by sharing with them what a successful piece of writing would look like. Ask children what they think about writing and ask them to show you a good piece of writing – are you both in agreement as to what writing is? By understanding more about the attitudes children have towards writing, it will help you as you begin to plan for writing across a range of subjects.

Most importantly, as you reflect on this chapter and think through what your planning may look like, you might wish to ask, how do I want pupils in my class to answer the question, '*Are you a good writer?*'

Concluding comments

As the author concludes this chapter she asks – 'Are you a good writer?' I would like to ask you – 'Are you a good teacher of writing?' This is a difficult question to answer as my own research has firmly established that teachers are not usually writers and that makes the teaching of writing very difficult. How can we confidently teach something that we are a little unsure of ourselves. There are, of course, many very skilled teachers who are writers and, for that matter, writers who are teachers. I would just like you to think this through as you continue your training and begin your teaching career.

Useful websites

www.everybodywrites.org.uk – resources for inspiring creative approaches to writing.

http://nationalstrategies.standards.dcsf.gov.uk/node/152632 – Talk for Writing resources.

CHAPTER 5

USING CHILDREN'S LITERATURE

JEAN WEBB

The author uses the following quote early on in this chapter:

> W.H. Davies wrote 'What is this life if full of care, We have no time to stand and stare'.

For me this offers the essence of this chapter, teaching is a busy, sometimes frantic activity which grows out of both the individual's and society's care for children. We want to ensure that each child enjoys their days in school, achieves their potential and ultimately leaves their primary years literate, numerate and feeling secure with their experience of this time.

The use of children's literature in the primary years allows some space for both teacher and child to 'stand and stare' not literally but metaphorically. We can see outside our world into the worlds of others – in both location and time. By teachers having knowledge of the academic field of children's literature, the potential of books for children can be realized. When reading this chapter, relax and revisit your own childhood reading and, most importantly, enjoy!

This chapter includes:

- an introduction to the study of children's literature
- children's literature and the construction of childhood
- children's literature for the primary school.

As a primary school teacher you may be wondering how the academic study of children's literature can be helpful to you and your students in the primary classroom, as such work may seem far away from the everyday practicalities of school life. I was an English, music and drama specialist and class teacher in primary schools for 17 years before joining the University of Worcester 20 years ago as a member of the English department. Then one of my responsibilities at Worcester was to teach a course on 'Children's Literature' to BEd students. This was an exciting and fascinating challenge, since the subject area of children's literature was then in its infancy in the UK. I certainly knew how literature could be employed in the classroom to engage children in story, poetry and drama to produce exhilarating and memorable experiences where all could succeed and learn more about themselves and the worlds around them. I also knew that literature could be used to bring to life other subjects such as history, geography and the sciences. I knew that children could learn and develop social skills, and increase in confidence, as I had witnessed this with the children I taught. They could also find a gateway into the imaginations of a myriad of authors, poets and dramatists, and open up and venture into their own imaginative landscapes. Through literature, language becomes more than a tool of literacy; it is the means by which we communicate with others and with ourselves.

The differences between a literary piece of writing and an 'ordinary' one are the ways in which the writer uses language to create images and experiences in the mind's eye of the reader so that one also feels, senses and learns new things; moreover the reader (both adult and child) is stimulated to think through their reading. Writers, in the widest sense, are important and powerful people. It is sobering to consider that writers and artists are those who are invariably targeted and silenced by totalitarian political regimes in order to ensure that their ideologies are neither threatened nor undermined through literary and artistic work that contains subversive thinking.

At this point you may well be thinking: 'This is rather too much for me! I am *only* working with children and reading to them from books written specifically for children and selecting books for the young to read themselves.' Yet, consider for a moment how and what you learnt and experienced from reading as a child. For my own part, being brought up in a working-class family in the post-war slum district of the East End of London in the 1950s, I remember luxuriating in Kenneth Grahame's descriptions of landscape in *The Wind in the Willows* (see the list of works cited at the end of this chapter) when Ratty and Mole venture out to find the lost baby otter, Little Portly, in the chapter

'The piper at the gates of dawn'. Ratty and Mole row along the river, searching through the long summer's night to look for Little Portly: 'In silence they landed, and pushed through the blossom and scented herbage and undergrowth that led up to the level ground, till they stood on a little lawn of marvellous green, set round with Nature's own orchard trees – crab-apple, wild cherry and sloe' (http://www.online-literature.com/view.php/windwillows/). The description read to me as of a Garden of Eden in rural England, far from the smoke stacks, factories, traffic and noise of the industrialized East End.

'"This is the place of my song-dream, the place the music played to me," whispered the Rat, as if in a trance' (http://www.online-literature.com/view. php/windwillows/). I would read this passage over and over as if entranced myself. Paradoxically, Grahame creates silence through his words, which then become those of the reader. The senses are activated and engaged; sight, smell and hearing are all brought into play. Play is an operative word here since reading great works of literature is a kind of 'play' where one can experiment, engage, experience and learn without even knowing that you are 'working' and also changing.

My other favourite book was Lewis Carroll's *Alice in Wonderland* (1864), because it did make me wonder at the strangeness of the world down the rabbit hole. I loved the word play and the puns, and trying to work out the puzzles. 'Reeling and writhing and fainting in coils' was a phrase which made me laugh when I 'translated' it into 'Reading and writing and painting in oils', not that painting in oils was anything that I would do until I was well into my fourth decade. The musical rhythm of the jokey sentence made it easy to learn and to enjoy saying aloud, and to feel the laughter in the words in my mouth. Also there was an uncomfortable strangeness about who Alice met, what happened to her, from shrinking to swim in her own pool of tears, to bursting out of a house as she grew to being a giant. As a child your body changes from month to month, and this can be disconcerting and almost worrying as you wonder whether you will be tall, short, middling, fat or slim. Also as I read and reread of the Cheshire cat I never did discover where it disappeared to, and why. But then, as a child, people and things do come and go and you do not know the reasons or the whereabouts. In a way one of the things I learnt was that you are not always going to find all of the answers, or solve all of the problems, and that you have to come to terms with knowing this. Life is always strange in some ways, especially to the child.

Task box

At this point you may wish to take a few moments to recall or think of a quotation, section of a book or perhaps a poem which has stayed with you from childhood because of the way in which the language is used, a way of capturing the moment, since as W.H. Davies wrote 'What is this life if full of care/ We have no time to stand and stare' (W.H. Davies, 1911).

One of the ways in which we can help children to dispel unnecessary strangenesses and to help them understand the world in which they live and where they may be in the futures they will make for themselves and for others, is to bring them the richness of learning and experiencing and feeling beyond the immediacy of their own moment through what literature can offer. The job of the academic studying children's literature is to make apparent and available to the non-specialist just what literature can do and what it has to offer.

An introduction to the study of children's literature

By now, I trust that you are curious as a reader to know what the study of children's literature can offer and what it can do to help you and the children you teach. However, the principal question which must arise in your mind, as one outside of academia, is exactly *what is* the study of children's literature? There is no simple singular answer to that question, except to say that academics think and write about literature for children from different perspectives. They use their own areas of expertise and their individual curiosities to pursue ranges of questions and puzzles. As one knows, simple questions lead to complex answers and a host of other questions. So, one starting question is 'where did the study of children's literature begin?'

There had been a level of interest in the late 1960s which has since burgeoned. In 1972, in America, Dr Francelia Butler founded the scholarly journal *Children's Literature: The Great Excluded*. This was a specialist academic journal and is important since it enabled the publication of serious works of criticism, and helped to establish the subject as being accepted in universities and higher education institutions. A year later the first Children's Literature Association (ChLA) meeting was held emanating from the group who had engaged with the idea of the journal. ChLA was founded to provide a meeting place for the serious discussion of books for children as literature and made a great stride in the development of children's literature as an academic subject. The ChLA now holds a large annual international conference in North America and publishes the *Children's Literature Association Quarterly and Children's Literature* which is 'the annual publication of the Children's Literature Association and the Modern Language Association Division on Children's Literature. The journal seeks to publish theoretically based articles that demonstrate an awareness of key issues and criticism in children's literature' (www.childlitassn.org/childrens_literature_journal. html). In addition these publications contain book reviews and information about activities and conferences in the field internationally. Recognition by the Modern Language Association means that children's literature is recognized as a bona fide academic subject, which is now taught worldwide in universities and higher education institutions. Doctorates are awarded in children's literature and there are also some professorships in the field.

Although the ChLA does attract international scholars, it is still principally a North American association focusing on texts and authors from the Americas.

The first colloquium of the International Research Association for Children's Literature (IRSCL) was held in Frankfurt leading to the full establishment of the society in 1970. The IRSCL is an extensively international association. They hold a conference every other year in different parts of the world. Their journal, *International Research in Children's Literature* was only founded in 2008, however, it plays an important part in bringing knowledge to readers and awareness of writing for children from many countries (www.irscl.com/about.html). Internationally the study of children's literature has expanded and strengthened over the past decade. The Australasian Children's Literature Association for Research came into being in the early 1990s and the Children's Literature Association, India, was founded *Circa* 2006. These are important developments which take the study of writing for children beyond the English speaking communities, and give a voice to marginalized and indigenous writers and scholars. In addition to the associations, which all run vibrant conferences, there are a few dedicated children's literature research centres internationally; namely, in the UK: the National Centre for Research in Children's Literature at the University of Roehampton (www.roehampton.ac.uk/researchcentres/ncrcl/); the International Centre for Research in Children's Literature, Literacy and Creativity at the University of Worcester (http://www.worc.ac.uk/businessandresearch/specialist/1014. html); and the Centre for International Research in Childhood: Literature, Culture, Media, at the University of Reading (www.rdg.ac.uk/circl/). In addition there is the 'Seven Stories' (www.sevenstories.org.uk/home/index.php) which is a museum attached to the University of Newcastle, which has a particular focus on links with children, schools and the community, and acts as an academic venue. Other centres internationally can be found in Cyprus, Osaka, South Africa, Stockholm and Sydney. Despite this great range of activity internationally there are still central questions which intrigued the early academics in the development of the field and which continue to be raised today.

Such questions are: what is children's literature and therefore, how do we define what is 'a children's book?' A simple answer is that a children's book is one which is *published* for children; yet this does not account for texts which cross over from adult literature to children's literature or vice versa (Beckett, 2008). The most well-known contemporary example of this phenomenon is J.K. Rowling's Harry Potter series. Furthermore, books for children can span wordless picture books for the very young to young adult fiction. To complicate matters further, picture books are not necessarily, and some would argue rarely, 'simple' texts. For example, Anthony Browne's *Willy's Pictures* (2002) makes sophisticated references to art history. Browne employs a surreal approach where imagination and reality slide over each other and become fused. His picture books make children look, wonder, laugh, think and try producing works of the Great Masters themselves. In addition to the complexity of picture books, the age range covered is extensive; from the pre-reader to the young adult and above. Graphic novels such as *Arkham Asylum: A Serious House on Serious Earth* (1989) by Grant Morrison and Dave McKean, which developed from the Batman comic, have made the transition from the genre of comics to sophisticated graphic novels which could still be classified in some ways as picture books. In short, what would seem to be a few simple questions raises a host of complex considerations which are directly pertinent to the work of the primary school teacher who is selecting books for children's reading and use in the classroom.

The debate over what is a children's book and what is suitable for children to read still continues, and will, I predict, continue to do so depending on which perspective one is coming from. The choices you make as a teacher in the UK reflect both your personal preferences, and very probably your moral, religious and political views within the framework of the National Curriculum and the particular school in which you are working, and the requirements of the children you are teaching.

Task box

At this point it would be an interesting exercise for you to jot down your thoughts as to what you consider to be the distinctive requirements of a book for children and what is suitable for children to read.

Perry Nodelman's *The Pleasures of Children's Literature* (1972) was an early and very influential text which suggested and discussed Perry's thoughts on what was a children's book. Some of his suggestions include the following, that:

- children's literature is simple and straightforward
- children's literature is optimistic
- children's literature tends towards fantasy.

One's initial response is to think that these look fine as unassailable statements, however, could one really say that Janet and Allan Ahlberg's *The Jolly Postman and Other People's Letters* (1986) is simple and straightforward? The great fun and challenge in this picture book for the very young onward is to make the links with other fairy stories and the world outside the land of fairy tale; to realize the jokes and to continue the possible stories. Pedagogically a great deal can be learned about letter writing. Furthermore there are moral considerations such as the Jolly Postman's illicit opening of other people's letters, and how we as the readers are implicated as we are complicit in this immoral act of an invasion of privacy.

The question of optimism is somewhat more difficult. Certainly not all books have happy endings, and some may have an inconclusive open ending such as Pamela Allen's *Black Dog* (1991). Allen's picture book tells the story of a little girl who lives in a cottage in a forest with her black dog. One day she sees an amazingly beautiful blue bird in a tree by the cottage. She is stunned by the bird's vibrant colouring; she is absorbed, fixated, obsessed and can only stand at the window hoping for another sighting of the bird. All through the winter she waits, putting out food for the bird and neglecting both herself and her faithful black dog. At last her own faithfulness is rewarded, for high in the tree is a movement and a figure comes flying from the branches. She thinks it is the blue bird, yet no, for it is her own black dog who has thrown himself from the height of the tree to fulfil her dreams. The final frame of the book is the child holding her black dog cradled in her arms. One is not sure whether he is alive or not; one hopes that he is sleeping: at least he looks happy and contented. Is the ending of this book optimistic? It is full of hope exuded by the reader who wants the dog to have survived. In another way it can be read as a story about optimism, for the child waits, hoping for the bird to return; yet in itself, in these circumstances hoping and dreaming life away is a sad loss. *Black Dog* is a fantasy, yet the faithfulness of some dogs is a reality. This seemingly simple story is a moral tale which implicitly criticizes wanting more than one has, for longing for the perfect experience, the ideal, and thereby wasting the moment and neglecting the love which is already there. These are real considerations in contemporary Western society when the drive is always to 'move on', 'gain more', to achieve your 'ideal home and lifestyle'. In the works of literary fantasy, reality is embedded, interwoven or paralleled in some way to make the reader or listener think.

If you now consider your own criteria for what constitutes a children's book I would suggest that you can raise many texts as exceptions to the 'rules' you have suggested.

Task box

Make a list of the criteria you would consider as defining a book for children, and then list those texts which comply and those which are exceptions.

Even subjects considered taboo 10 or 20 years ago are being included in serious writing for children. Death, sexuality, incest, abuse, gay and lesbian relationships, and the inclusion of natural bodily functions, for example, can all be read about by children, perhaps not explicitly in texts for younger children, but they can be variously identified. This raises the question in a slightly different way about what is suitable for children. Such judgements have changed over time and vary according to the cultural context. Nicholas Tucker's *Suitable for Children?* (1976), very clearly sets out the arguments which have influenced English children's literature concerning suitability for younger readers. He traces such central moral debates back to the nineteenth century when women writers such as Mrs Trimmer and Mrs Sherwood, who emanated from the Sunday School movement, were voicing their concerns for the moral health of the young. They thought fairy tales to be an immoral and dark influence on children. This may seem somewhat extreme from a modern perspective, yet their centrally Christian moral positioning reflected a sense of responsibility for the young in a social context where children received very little education either formally or morally; where children were working in factories and mines from a very young age and exposed to the harshness and wickednesses associated with poverty, depravity and alcoholism. Fairy tales at that time were very different from the seemingly harmless tales for young children they are regarded as today. The nineteenth-century tales were salacious and violent versions published for adults in cheap pamphlet editions, or chap books available from pedlars. (For further information see, for example, Jack Zipes, 1979, *Breaking the Magic Spell*.) Fantasy as a literary form was regarded by the women writers of the Sunday School Movement as harmful, since it would, in their view, distract children from thinking about the realities of their lives. Writing for children was, principally, to be didactic and educative. On the other hand, others, such as Charles Dickens, argued for fairy tales and fantasy to be a central part of reading for children, and for adults. He stated that:

> In an utilitarian age, of all other times, it is a matter of grave importance that Fairy tales should be respected … every one who has considered the subject knows full well that a nation without fancy, without some romance, never did, never can, never will hold a great place under the sun. (Tucker, 1976: 48)

Charles Dickens is certainly making his own strong views felt about the need for literature to entertain, to open and create worlds of fantasy and imagination; he is also implicitly making a strong statement about the relationship between writing for children and the senses of national and cultural identity.

This point opens up this discussion of the study of children's literature into the wider areas which are researched and written about by academics. Writing for children is not the same in every country but reflects the cultural and national constructions embedded in literature for children. Children's literature can be understood as an integral part of the cultural system which creates and sustains the culture, society or nation. For example, literature for children under the Soviet system was very carefully and closely controlled. Those who wrote for children were vetted by the state; both publishers and writers had to adhere to the Soviet ideal both in their own thinking and behaviour and in what they produced. Stories for children were principally written in a realist mode or were versions of traditional fairy tales. In all these texts characters and plots were not allowed to deviate from the perfect Party line. Mare Mursepp, an Estonian academic, has edited an enlightening and thought-provoking collection of essays called *The Sunny Side of Darkness*: *Children´s Literature in Totalitarian and Post-Totalitarian Eastern Europe* (2005) in which academics from the former German Democratic Republic, the Soviet states, the Czech Republic, Estonia and Latvia, for example, discuss the ways in which children's literature was central to the Soviet political project. This collection of essays and other work by scholars in children's literature makes it very apparent that children's literature is never an 'innocent' means of communication. (See, for example, John Stephens's *Language and Ideology in Children's Fiction*, 1992).

Task box

It would be an enlightening exercise here for you, as a teacher, to note the texts which you use as recommended by the National Literacy Strategy, and to identify how far and in which ways they reflect culture, nationality, class and particular values.

Children's literature and the construction of childhood

A great deal of research has taken place and been published over the past 15 years which reads writing for children within the contexts of social and cultural studies. In order for such work to be carried out in terms of 'placing' and understanding children's literature within cultural contexts an understanding of the historical context and development of writing for children has to be established. Initially such work emanated from two sets of writers: those interested in book collecting and antique books, and biographers who were focusing on particular authors. For example, the work of Eric Quayle on collecting children's books is a very useful introduction to books for children from the seventeenth century onward (Quayle, 1971). Early biographies such as Humphrey Carpenter's *Secret Gardens* (1985) were snapshots of the lives of charismatic children's authors such as Lewis Carroll, J.M. Barrie and Kenneth Grahame. Early biographies focused on the more enigmatic aspects of the authors' lives and also bordered on interest in the perhaps more salacious circumstances of their biographies. These works are interesting as far as they go, however, more recent studies have paid far more attention to the literary and cultural aspects of the writing and the context in which the work was produced. Morton Cohen's biography of Lewis Carroll (1995), for example, is a fascinating work which sets Dodgson fully within the worlds of nineteenth century Oxford and London where the writer was living, working and enjoying the social life of the capital. Cohen also goes further to consider the literary aspects of Dodgson's work, for example, the influence of mathematics and logic upon Dodgson/Lewis Carroll's fantasy writing for children.

To write a comprehensive history of English children's literature is a mammoth task. Today there are over 7,000 books for children published each year in the UK, not taking account of children's books which are in English and published outside the UK. There has also been an established publishing industry in Britain since the mid-nineteenth century. What has been very successfully achieved is a collective history of English children's literature produced independently by different scholars. John Rowe Townsend's ground-breaking *Written for Children* (1965) gives a very readable overview of the development of writing for children from before 1840 to about 1985. He divides his historical account by themes, such as fantasy, the adventure story and picture books. Townsend gives an invaluable overview which demonstrates the relationship between history, the subject matter of children's literature and, implicitly, politics. For example, the adventure story in the nineteenth century was very much aimed at boys to stir their imaginations for venturing as explorers and heroes to further the glory and achievements of the British Empire. Following on from Townsend, Peter Hunt has written and edited a number of, again, invaluable books on the history of, and areas to consider when studying, children's literature, such as *An Introduction to Children's Literature* (1994) and *Children's Literature: An Illustrated History* (Hunt, 1995). These works really do form an invaluable base for the understanding of work which delves more deeply into the effects of the publishing industry (Reynolds and Tucker, 2006) and cultural and social development as reflected by authors for children, as in Kimberley Reynolds's *Radical Children's Literature* (2007). This latest award-winning book exposes and analyses the ways in which writing for children demonstrates the radical changes and challenges contemporary British society is undergoing and clearly proves that children's literature is a central influence on how we live and think in Britain today. Writers of young adult and teenage fiction are, for example, raising questions about and discussing drug abuse, self-harming, the changing role and construction of the family, and what it is like to live in multicultural Britain in the twenty-first century. What histories of writing for children demonstrate is how we have changed in our thinking over the centuries about writing for children, what is suitable for them to read and how our culture and society itself has changed.

By reading differing approaches to the history of children's literature, which are all written in an available and readable style, you can, as a teacher, understand how and why writing for children has changed and bring that richness of knowledge into your classroom by discussing the context and generation of work with your students. What one does clearly realize in reading varying approaches to histories of children's literature is that a central area for consideration is how childhood and the construction of the notion of the child itself has changed and how such is reflected in, and influenced by, children's literature. Children's literature has played its own part in literary thinking, being influenced by Romanticism from the late eighteenth century to the late nineteenth century and Modernism from the early twentieth century to the 1980s when Postmodernism came into the thinking of writers and the conceptualization of experience.

From the late eighteenth century to the late nineteenth century Romanticism was a dominant mode of thinking. The model of the child, therefore, reflected and was constructed upon the conceptualization of the Romantic thinkers and writers. William Blake and William Wordsworth, among others, had an idealized notion of the child, which they embedded in their writing. The Romantic child is open to learning; moving from innocence to experience; having a close emotive relationship with nature and the landscape, and developing new thinking and experiences through worlds of the imagination. The view of the child as being essentially innocent has had a great influence upon our culture, as has that journey from innocence to experience.

Modernism shifted from the certainties and idealism of the nineteenth century to the post-First World War era when that confidence that one could have all the answers disintegrated in the radical aftermath of the devastation on the battlefields. Writers could no longer always conclude their work with happy closed endings and the confidence of being able to answer all questions. This was true across Europe and also in America, for example, in E.B. White's *Charlotte's Web* (1952). White leaves the reader with a sense of disappointment with Fern who abandons Wilbur, now her prize-winning pig, to spend time with a new-found boyfriend as she enters adolescence and rides on the Ferris wheel, which symbolizes a new turning in her life. Wilbur has to learn to live without Charlotte his mentor. He does have Charlotte's offspring, but it is Wilbur who now has to take over responsibility for his own life with the knowledge that perhaps none of the baby spiders will have Charlotte's facility with language which has guided Wilbur and given him self-confidence. Writing for children was beginning to reflect the influences of more complex approaches to childhood and a greater sense of exploration of the inner life of the mind and the thinking post-Freud et al. There was also a growing awareness from the turn of the century of the sense of the fracturing and multiplicity of the self. Rudyard Kipling's Kim (1901), for example, questions who he is when the Llama, his guide through life, is not with him. The child per se was realized as being more complex and reflecting the psychological states recognized in the adult.

The later stages of the twentieth century were influenced by Postmodernism, where the subject self is realized as being decidedly complex and multiple, as living in western society demands differing responses from the self, rather than the singular unchanging character that one would have read in say an Enid Blyton story of the 1950s. The way in which authors including children's authors wrote reflected this complexity by the use of time shifts and different forms within the text, such as flashbacks, diaries, and extracts from newspapers etc. A ludic quality in the writing also emerged which made the reader very much aware that the texts and the relationship with the author is in itself an artifice. Philip Pullman's *Clockwork* (1997) playfully experiments with form in his pastiche of a German fairy tale by incorporating several narratives within the text. What one realises is that the whole of this complex plot will hinge upon the hero tripping over a cat thus catapulting a cause and effect narrative into motion. Jon Scieszka and Lane Smith also typify this playful approach in their revision of fairytales in their picture book *The Stinky Cheeseman* (1992). They have, for example, the character of Jack (of Beanstalk fame) who is the narrator and directly enters the text by making it evident that he is, like a pastiche of a 1930s movie producer, trying to get a book 'on the road'. The fairy tales are retold in a very humorous and witty style which debunks the fantasy and magic of fairy tales. The Ugly Duckling, a relation of Hans Andersen's creation no doubt, turns out to be an ugly duck, never to become the swan, while the Frog will not transform into a Prince, but rather enjoy the kiss of the unsuspecting, yet hopeful, Princess.

The *Bildungsroman*, or novel of experience, originating in Germany in the latter part of the eighteenth century, charts the journey of development both physical and psychological, and is a major form which underpins English, European and American literature. By the end of the novel the protagonist is changed, having learned a great deal through their physical, psychological and emotional journeying. This form and approach to the perception and development of childhood is still dominant in contemporary writing for children. For example, Harry Potter undergoes considerable changes as he learns more about his origins, himself and the two worlds in which he lives; while Lyra in Philip Pullmans' trilogy, His Dark Materials, changes from being 'a little savage' in *Northern Lights* (1997), wandering and fighting her way through the corridors of Jordan College and the streets of Oxford, to being the young woman who has travelled through many worlds and learnt a great deal about life and herself, so that she will be the visionary who will make the new 'New Republic of Heaven' at the end of *The Amber Spyglass* (2000).

Perhaps we do not question the expectation that our children will learn and change as it is so embedded in our Western cultural approach that it is now invisible, yet literature which demonstrates and engages with change actually teaches this to our child readers. Indian literature for children, for example, has, until recently, principally been comprised of retellings of traditional stories which do not contemplate change, nor involve the child protagonist or reader as an active participant; they require that the tradition is learnt and continued. But what are the implications of change and evolution, for such expectations as innocence built into the Romantic construction of the child?

Frances Hodgson Burnett's *Little Lord Fauntleroy* (1886) is the story of an innocent and innately good child who manages to heal the rift between the aristocratic English branch of his family typified by his crusty grandfather and the American democratic side as embodied in his gentle mother. The 'problem' with Little Lord Fauntleroy, as Victor Watson (1996) has pointed out, is that he is so good that no child could emulate this paragon of perfection. The figure of Fauntleroy was so influential at the turn of the nineteenth century that little boys (including my father and uncles) were dressed in velvet suits in the Fauntleroy style and wore the long ringlets which adorned the head of the angelic child. In the late twentieth century the Jamie Bulger case, when two boys brutally murdered a young child, horrifically raised the question as to whether children could be 'innocent', or whether they could be 'born evil'. Anne Fine's subtle and disturbing novel *The Tulip Touch* (1997) interrogates this premise and asks some further disturbing questions such as who was really responsible for the demonic behaviour of Tulip, the child herself, the parents or society? Other writers such as Jacqueline Wilson continue to ask uncomfortable questions of contemporary British culture. In Wilson's *Illustrated Mum* (1999) for example, the two young sisters are 'adult' and responsible, taking care of both themselves and their mother who suffers from a bipolar mental disorder. Texts such as these, works of literature, which engage the reader, create the world and the context within the imagination so that the reader can think through and puzzle about situations, and therefore going much further than books which deal with social 'issues' in a simplistic and reductive manner. Literature employs the skills and the literary imagination of the writer to create complex and multidimensional reading experiences. Michael Morpurgo, for example, in *Private Peaceful* (2004) could have been said to have been writing about the tragic scandal of men in the First World War who were executed as cowards, yet had in reality been ill, suffering from shellshock. Morpurgo had at that time, been involved in the campaign to bring this travesty to the attention of the government and to have the records of men who had been executed changed to recognize their true condition and patriotic relationship to Britain. *Private Peaceful* is not a piece of propaganda, but a subtle and sensitively told story which takes the reader into the lives and understanding of the time and the experiences of these young men, not more than boys themselves, who were on the battlefields and in the trenches. The novel includes a poignant diary, flashbacks, childhood recollections, love stories, adventures, and the stories of families and lives torn asunder by war, with soldiers, officers and people caught in situations which were tragically beyond their individual control. Children's literature is an art form executed at the highest level, which engages with the child reader, the child and childhood as the principal subject.

> ## Task box
>
> At this point it would be an interesting exercise for you, as the reader and disseminator of texts and reading to children, to note your personal components of the construction of childhood. What do you perceive to be important? Which books and authors convey, or fail to convey, these? Does your construction of the child and childhood match with what you are doing and are required to do in your professional life?

The literary construction of the child is a subject which has received a great deal of academic attention, particularly in the areas of feminist and gender studies. Such attention has both reflected in and contributed to debates. Christine Wilkie-Stibbs, for example, in *The Feminine Subject in Children's Literature* (2002) draws upon contemporary literary theory and feminist theory to give an insightful discussion of the ways in which the depiction of girls has been shaped and constructed since the nineteenth century. There are many other fine scholars who have been working in this subject area and who have made valuable contributions to raising the awareness of readers. As a female child reader in the 1950s, if I wanted tales of high adventure and travel I had to read stories and novels written for boys such as R.M. Ballantyne's *Coral Island* (1858), Robert Louis Stevenson's *Treasure Island* (1883), or adventure comics such as *The Wizard* or *Hotspur*. Books for girls at that time were set in the home, the genre of domestic fiction typified by Louisa May Alcott's *Little Women* (1868) or Susan Coolidge's *What Katy Did* (1871). Adventuring girls in England had to take on a masculine persona such as Georgie in Enid Blyton's adventures. The whole awareness of gender inequality and difference was gently, humorously and intelligently brought into children's awareness through fiction by Anne Fine in *Bill's New Frock* (1989). Fine puts a boy into the body of a girl and then follows his tribulations and discoveries as he experiences, as it were, life on the other side.

> When Bill Simpson woke up on Monday morning, he found he was a girl … Forced off to school in a frilly pink dress, Bill discovers one of the worst days in his life is about to begin … Baffled by the way things are just *different* for girls, Bill falls headlong into trouble. As the amazing day drags on, Bill's new frock becomes dirtier and tattier. How will it all end for him – or her? (http://www.annefine.co.uk/books/billsfrock.php)

The consciousness of the construction of childhood in children's literature encompasses a wide spectrum. Aidan Chambers poignantly and sensitively explores and presents the world of an adolescent boy in his novel *Dance On My Grave* (1982). Hal encounters his homosexuality, yet this is not the problematic situation for him, but the difficulties of dealing with his own and his lover's demanding personalities. At the time Chambers used a particularly experimental Postmodern form which was to combine different types of text and discourse into the novel. For example, there are newspaper cuttings, diary entries, the notebooks entries from Hal's social worker, as well as clips from song lyrics and the thoughts circulating in Hal's mind. This mode of writing depicts the crowded life of Hal who is at a stage in his life when what others have to say dominates him, until he can reach a stage of maturity and adulthood and control his own life. What the book captures especially well is the obsessive nature of love, especially love in adolescence, and the evolution of dynamic personalities. Essentially literature for children is not afraid to deal with major issues and problems with the central focus and locus of exploration being the child and the world of child experience.

The central point here is that if one understands how texts work then one is far better placed to teach others to read and write effectively. It is also about understanding thinking processes and problem solving. *Bill's New Frock* caused a great stir and has continued to raise conversation because the reversal of roles was an excellent way in which to enable and to position the reader into considering gender as a social construction. It was a simple transition, yet made explicit what was buried beneath convention and social norms. A book can change a life. What once was imagined can well become reality.

However, what is reality for one child differs radically from that of another. Children can deeply learn about different realities through reading because literary texts can make what they read come to life. Historical fiction enables an immediacy in the recreation of bygone times. Nina Bawden's *Carrie's War* (1973), for example, vividly depicts the experiences of children evacuated during the Second World War, as does Michelle Magorian's *Goodnight, Mr. Tom* (1983) In both texts the children are dislocated and thus encounter different parts of the country from war-torn London; they also mix with different social classes, and have to adapt to rural life. Multicultural literature, for example, the excellent work which is coming from British Asian writers, such as Angela Jariwala, brings the awareness of other cultural experiences in contemporary Britain to the reader. In Jariwala's young adolescent novel, *Fatty Rati* (1997), the heroine is British Asian and adolescent. She has the same concerns as the majority of teenage girls in Britain irrespective of racial background: her figure; her friendships; whether she will ever get a boyfriend; clothes; her future and what she wants to do (i.e. no real idea!) and what her parents want her to do (i.e. be sensible, work hard, get a good education). Unfortunately in common with a growing percentage of the British populace she is overweight. There is thus a core of commonality of what it is to 'be' a teenager, in addition Jariwala combines this touching story of teenage angst with the experiences of being a British Asian. Food is important in the story, not only because of Rati's problems, but because it is a cultural indicator denoting the Indianness of the cultural experience. Through her storytelling Jariwala discusses eating disorders, marriage expectations for both sexes and how individuals are socialized into gender roles, and the problems arising; plus approaches to family life and the expectations of the extended Asian family pattern. Interestingly the novel also includes the differentiation between various sectors of the British Asian population itself, such as those from Pakistan and those from South India. Through reading, children can learn and absorb an understanding of different cultures which are part of their own, yet potentially so distant. Reading can bridge cultural distance to formulate multicultural awareness and enable understanding. Children's literature can be a powerful force.

Children's literature for the primary classroom

Uncle Tom's Cabin was the first book to sell a million copies: a nineteenth-century block-buster; it was big business. The contemporary children's book market is also a multimillion pound industry with, for example, J.K. Rowling's Harry Potter phenomenon and the success of Philip Pullman's trilogy, His Dark Materials, both of which have been published in adult editions, where the text remains the same, and only the book covers have been changed to appeal to the adult eye. In one way this is certainly all positive, in another it can paradoxically lead to a paucity of knowledge about books since these market leaders dominate, potentially eclipsing the wealth of other texts which do not achieve such recognition, success and the benefits of enormously expensive marketing budgets and being made into highly successful films, with all of the associated commercial spin-offs. Some recent research, which is worrying to contemplate, indicated that although teachers are aware of an acceptable range of authors they only introduce a very small number to their students.

> When asked to list 6 'good' children's writers, responses indicate that a wide number of authors are known to primary practitioners, although quite a few listed here might be more readily seen as picturebook makers. 64% of the teachers named five or six writers. 46% named six. Roald Dahl gained the highest number of mentions by far (744). The nearest four were: Michael Morpurgo (343), Jacqueline Wilson (323), JK Rowling (300) and Anne Fine (252). Others above a hundred mentions were: Dick King Smith (172), Janet and Alan Ahlberg (169), Enid Blyton (161), Shirley Hughes (128), CS Lewis (122), Philip Pullman (117), Mick Inkpen (106) and Martin Waddell (100). (Cremin et al., 2008: 4)

The pressures of time on teachers emanating from the requirements of the National Curriculum could be blamed, since it is easier to reach for the well-known, with easy success and ready availability rather than bring in new or lesser publicized works. There is also the widely based practice of using extracts from books rather than the whole text. In terms of teaching the joys of reading literature and employing literacy skills for what they are intended for, that is to read, enjoy and learn through books, such approaches and practices amount to intellectual and social 'criminality'. New writers cannot survive without a reading public, and neither can texts by established and lesser-known writers which do not achieve certain levels of readership. Print runs of children's books, other than the block-busters are shockingly small. An average print run will be around 1,000 to 1,500 books because of printing and storage costs. Therefore a book can disappear from print before it has achieved recognition. So who are these writers, and where, might you ask, can we find out about and obtain work other than that of the best-known authors? Fortunately there are excellent resources in the UK to support you. Over the past 20 years the number of awards for children's books has increased, and these include awards for new writers. The results of these competitions will also include the shortlisted books and authors. Excellent sites such as The Book Trust keep back-lists of award and shortlists, so that one can quickly develop a bank of knowledge. Journals such as *Books For Keeps, Children's Literature in Education* and *The Lion and the Unicorn* publish book reviews, as do librarianship journals and magazines. The Internet is a great source of information, with online bookshops which give access to literature from around the world. We are no longer limited to the high street bookshops, which carry a very limited, range because it does not suit their economic policies to do otherwise. Furthermore, literature from other countries does not often appear in the British high street bookshops. Whereas in Iceland, Sweden, Finland, Denmark and Germany, for example, there is a wealth of texts translated from other languages, in the UK this is sadly not so. The block comes from the major British and British American publishing houses which are unwilling to pay for the costs of translation. Even books from Ireland and Australia, where the children's writers for all ages of readers produce exciting and mind-blowingly imaginative literature, rarely appear in British shops. However, there is the Internet. The world is open to the young reader who is always ready to explore, but they do need a guide, and that responsibility lies principally with the teacher. All you need is a key to the resources which are out there, and then you can follow your own trails of exploration. As the teacher you are the facilitator, the disseminator and, of course, the reader.

Not only do you have support of the academic community but you also have the excellent support of the Children's Laureate. There have been five Laureates to date who are elected as champions of children's literature and must have made an outstanding contribution to the literary world of children's books. Their job is to promote reading with children and to excite and inform adults and children.

With all of this adult interest in reading and literature for children, it is essential that the child reader is not overlooked. After all, they are the ones who should be at the heart of the experience, yet it is easy not to listen to them, or to even ask them what they really think. The practice of literary criticism, that is, saying how and what and why you think and feel about the book you have read, and the things it makes you think about outside of the story is a fundamental part of the process of reading, yet is often neglected. In one way it *is why* the author writes the book in the first place, to have an effect and induce a reaction in the reader. So, we should ask children to talk about what they have read in a way that they wish to talk about it, rather than respond to directive questions which result in the answers we want to hear. Work conducted by Webb and Cox (2010) has explored the idea of using children as literary critics by taking children's writers' draft works directly to students to have them provide feedback and comments about how they think the story is developing. This has proved very insightful for all concerned in the project as the huge children's literature publishing industry has seldom before utilized the opinions of its consumers to gauge the potential success of a book.

In conclusion, the knowledge which you have as a teacher enables you to bring other worlds and other lives and understanding into the experience of the children you teach. The more you learn and know, the more you can give to the younger generations and the greater success you will have in the very important work which you do which educates children and creates the future. You are a reader, a learner and a facilitator of knowledge, and in some ways an interpreter. Scholars variously studying children's literature have, and continue to provide, a wealth of knowledge for you which lies beneath and behind texts and shapes reading matter and the experience of reading itself. The more you read and learn, the more you can give. So at this point I shall leave you to your new reading and exploration.

Concluding comments

Now you have read this chapter I would be interested in your thoughts on one of the roles that the author gives you in the final section – she suggests that you will be interpreters of children's literature to your pupils. What exactly does this mean? Will you tell them the stories? Will you introduce them to the author and the authors' work? What does interpreter mean? I like the suggestion that interpreter means 'exponent or advocate' – you will be responsible for presenting this rich world to your pupils and inviting them into it – just as the White Rabbit does in *Alice in Wonderland*; Lucy does to her siblings in *The Lion, the Witch and the Wardrobe*; and perhaps even take on the role that Platform 9¾ does at Kings Cross Station in the Harry Potter series.

Literary works cited in this chapter

| Hans Christian Andersen | 1844 | *The Ugly Duckling* |
| R.M. Ballantyne | 1858 | *Coral Island* |

Lewis Carroll	1864	*Alice in Wonderland*
Louisa May Alcott	1868	*Little Women*
Susan Coolidge	1871	*What Katy Did*
Robert Louis Stevenson	1883	*Treasure Island*
Frances Hodgson Burnett	1886	*Little Lord Fauntleroy*
Rudyard Kipling	1901	*Kim*
Kenneth Grahame	1908	*The Wind in the Willows*
W.H. Davies	1911	*Leisure*
E.B. White	1952	*Charlotte's Web*
Nina Bawden	1973	*Carrie's War*
Aidan Chambers	1982	*Dance On My Grave*
Michelle Magorian	1983	*Goodnight, Mr. Tom*
Janet and Allan Ahlberg	1986	*The Jolly Postman and Other People's Letters*
Grant Morrison and Dave McKean	1989	*Arkham Asylum: A Serious House on Serious Earth*
Anne Fine	1989	*Bill's New Frock*
Pamela Allen	1991	*Black Dog*
Jon Scieszka and Lane Smith	1992	*The Stinky Cheeseman*
Philip Pullman	1996	*Clockwork*
J.K. Rowling	1997	*Harry Potter and the Philosopher's Stone*
Philip Pullman	1997	*Northern Lights*
Anne Fine	1997	*The Tulip Touch*
Jariwala	1997	*Fatty Rati*
J.K. Rowling	1998	*Harry Potter and the Chamber of Secrets*
J.K. Rowling	1999	*Harry Potter and the Prisoner of Azkaban*

Jaqueline Wilson	1999	*Illustrated Mum*
J.K. Rowling	2000	*Harry Potter and the Goblet of Fire*
Philip Pullman	2000	*The Amber Spyglass*
Anthony Browne	2002	*Willy's Pictures*
J.K. Rowling	2003	*Harry Potter and the Order of the Phoenix*
Michael Morpurgo	2004	*Private Peaceful*
J.K. Rowling	2005	*Harry Potter and the Half-Blood Prince*
J.K. Rowling	2007	*Harry Potter and the Deathly Hallows*

ORGANIZING LEARNING AND TEACHING LITERACY

CHAPTER 6

LANGUAGE, LITERACY AND ICT

BOB FOX

Only five to ten years ago in teacher education we spent time in information and communication technology (ICT) classes focusing on developing student skills in using ICT. However, now, as we have more students in initial teacher education who grew up with the National Curriculum in place, these skills are firmly acquired throughout Key Stages 1–4 in school. In fact, most of you reading this book as an undergraduate textbook will be 'digital natives' – you need to read the chapter to find out what this means.

Information and communication technology in primary classrooms these days often means talking about the use of the interactive whiteboard (IWB) and the nature of the best pedagogical fit for lessons and IWB work. However, this chapter takes up some of the not so glamorous aspects of English and ICT in the primary classrooms, which will prove very useful to those beginning to train as teachers.

> **This chapter includes:**
>
> - writing with a computer
>   - keyboarding
>   - word processing
> - using the interactive whiteboard
> - multimodel literacy
> - talking stories
> - using the Internet
> - blogs, wikis and email
> - podcasting.

Background

Computers have had a place in UK primary classrooms since about 1982, so by now we should have got past thinking of them as something new. If you are under 30 years of age, the probability is that you grew up with computers at schools and perhaps at home, and you are what is often referred to as a *digital native* (Prensky, 2001) – in other words, computers have always been part of the world you know and recognize. On the other hand, many older teachers (and people who devise the school curriculum) are *digital immigrants* – in other words, they have had to adapt their world view to accommodate the idea of computer technology. Because you are young, older teachers will expect you to know all about new technologies. Do not disappoint their expectations!

What computers are capable of doing, and how we conceptualize what they are *for*, have both evolved considerably over time, and will continue to do so. We have moved from one per school to one per class, and are now rapidly approaching one per child. We have moved on from small memory and storage, slow processors, low-resolution graphics, monochrome printing and relatively high unit costs; interactive whiteboards are now to be found in most (though not all) primary classrooms – and what we currently use will all look terribly slow and primitive in another decade's time. In most classrooms a range of digital technologies apart from computers can be made available. A large majority of primary school children now have access to computers and the Internet at home. In many cases they have much better equipment than is available to them at school, and it has been estimated that, on average, the amount of time they spend on a home computer is four times the amount spent on one at school (Becta, 2002). Much of that time may be spent playing games, but for many children the volume and complexity of reading and writing they do at their home computer considerably exceeds what they do *in total* at school. Teachers, on the whole, know very little about the ICT experience and competences that children gain at home (see, for example, Marsh et al., 2005; McPake et al., 2004). To ignore ICT in the teaching of literacy would be extremely foolish.

The Rose Review (Rose, 2009) places ICT firmly within the core of the primary curriculum. The *affordances* of ICT enable the advancement of learning in ways that are in some respects significantly better than what was possible in the past. What needs to be clearly understood is that good pedagogy in relation to ICT is not different from good pedagogy underpinning good literacy teaching generally. It is not a case of using ICT as a 'bolt-on extra' to literacy teaching – teachers who say 'It's hard enough teaching literacy, without having to teach ICT at the same time' have significantly missed the point.

- ICT is not merely a reward – 'I've finished my work, Miss – can I play on the computer?'
- ICT is not an afterthought, or merely a way of prettifying children's work – 'I've finished my writing, Miss – can I type it up on the computer?' There *are* circumstances in which this would be appropriate. We will return to this point later.
- Do not use ICT just because it is there, and do not use it merely because you know you are supposed to. When planning a lesson, think through the ways in which ICT can improve what you are trying to do. If there really are none, then do not use it.

High Street shops sell software for home use, intended to help children with literacy. Almost without exception these contain low-level drill-and-practice exercises and tests. These miss the point almost entirely, have no place in the primary classroom, and should not be endorsed by teachers, except possibly occasionally as a form of reinforcement. Their main crime is that they confuse teaching with testing.

As a general rule, software is pedagogically useful if it places the child in control (see, for example, Cook and Finlayson, 1999). It is a quite easy distinction – is the software doing what the child wants, or is the child doing what the software wants?

Much current thinking about effective pedagogy is based on the work of Vygotsky (see Chapters 1, 2 and 3 for an outline of this pedagogical stance).

Writing with a computer 1: keyboarding

It is quite distressing to see a Year 5 or 6 child running an index finger backwards and forwards across a keyboard looking for a letter, 'pecking at keys'. By that age more or less every child should be able to work quickly and efficiently with a keyboard. To be unable to do so represents an enormous waste of their time. Whatever we think about the QWERTY keyboard layout, it has defied all attempts to replace it, so that is what children will need to get used to (voice-activated software notwithstanding). By the time they reach adolescence most children have been engaged in some sort of online chat-room activity, for the effective use of which fast typing is normally a prerequisite. We owe it to children to give them some help in developing good keyboard habits.

Task box

- How quickly can you type the letters A–Z? (If you are on Facebook, try http://apps.facebook.com/typea-z/. You will probably not be able to access Facebook via a school network, but children could time each other with the aid of a stopwatch.)
- What is a good time? Can children improve on their best times?
- Perhaps rather more purposefully than simply typing the alphabet, you could provide a couple of sentences or a short verse for children to type out without errors.
- Observe them – do they watch the screen, the keyboard or both?

Some early years teachers are exercised by the fact that keyboards conventionally display capital letters, and much early literacy work in schools concentrates on lower-case letters only. It is possible to buy lower-case keyboards, or sets of stickers to put on keys. After a while stickers tend to come loose and move around, making the keys sticky, grubby and perhaps unhealthy. A cursory glance at the environmental print that surrounds children in the wider world amply demonstrates that it is unrealistic to expect children to interact with lower-case letters only; for most the capitals on the keys represent a problem for a very short period of time, if at all. A reasonable compromise might be keys displaying both lower and upper case. There is an apocryphal story about an early years teacher who thought her children would not cope with the QWERTY keyboard, so she pulled all the keys off and put them back in alphabetical order …

From the start children should be encouraged to type with both hands, with as many fingers as they feel comfortable using, but in any case more than one on each hand, as a means of minimizing the risk of repetitive strain injury (RSI). Touch-typing is perhaps desirable, and there are many software tutors available, but it should not be attempted with children whose hands are not yet big enough to cover the keys appropriately.

Children will need to learn how to space the words they write by the use of the space bar. Some early years children put a finger on the screen and hit the space bar several times until they have created a 'finger space'. Tell them not to.

Children should be familiar with the keyboard locations of letters, numbers and the basic punctuation marks they are likely to use. They should know how to use the shift key to obtain capitals and so forth. They should know how to use the shift lock to create, for example, headings. *Do not* teach them to lock and unlock the shift lock every time they want a capital letter – if they are used to using two hands there should not be a problem. They should also know how to use the Return or Enter key to start a new line.

They should know how to use the Delete and Backspace keys to remove unwanted things, and how to highlight words and blocks of text to delete, copy or move text. Encourage children to use the keyboard shortcuts, particularly Ctrl-C and Ctrl-V to copy and paste, as these are usually the most efficient ways of conducting these operations. They should also, of course, know how to load and save their work, and how to print it. If the printer does not spring to life instantly, less experienced children sometimes hit the Print option several times, to 'help it on its way'.

Writing with a computer 2: word processing

There are some excellent word processors available which are customized for use by primary school children; on the other hand, probably the majority of children have access to Microsoft Word at home. The suggestion here is that a good primary classroom should have both available. The essential difference is that the primary word processors have what has been called a 'pedagogic layer' – they are intended to teach – whereas Word is intended for use by people who already know how to use it. You will need to think clearly about the context in which the word processor is to be used, in order to determine which would be most appropriate.

The most important thing to understand is that there is a difference between writing by hand and writing with a word processor. First, when you write by hand you need to think out exactly what you are going to write long before you actually write it, otherwise you need to cross out or rub out every time you change your mind, whereas with a word processor you can work heuristically and amend what you are saying as you go along, without leaving any untidy marks. Second, when you have finished writing something by hand and need or wish to redraft it, you have to write the whole thing again, including those parts that are to remain unaltered (which children universally detest), whereas with a word processor you merely change the things you wanted to change. The word-processed text can be reformatted in a different font, or blocks of text can be added or copied and pasted elsewhere. You can produce multiple printouts, email files or post them to the Web. Most of this is fairly self-evident to anyone who is used to doing it, of course, but it does not customarily feature strongly in literacy lessons.

There is more to it than that. When children write by hand, they have to consider letter formation, joining, spelling, neatness of handwriting, and a whole range of transcription issues that do not strictly have any bearing on the content of what they are writings, Chapter 7 discusses these in detail. Over the years teachers have told children they are interested in content and ideas, but have expressed most of their judgements in relation to transcription issues. One consequence is that children tend to be conservative in what they write, for example, by choosing words they know how to spell. The word processor helps to scaffold the writing process by taking away all the handwriting issues, and if a spellchecker is in use, it enables children to be more adventurous in what they write, in the knowledge that it is all malleable. Of course, if you wish to assess children's spelling accuracy, you need to make your judgements on pieces of work written without the aid of a spellchecker.

As long as some children know what they are doing, you do not need to teach the basics of word processing to everyone in a systematic manner. If children work collaboratively at a word processor, in twos or threes, a lot of peer-tutoring can happen. You need to ensure that children take it in turns to be the typist, otherwise the one who needs the most practice will get the least. Other roles might be the 'thinkist', who suggests the form of words to be used, and the editor, who watches the screen for errors, and suggests alternatives.

Given the chance, children will spend hours experimenting with different fonts (this is sometimes referred to as 'fontitis'), and end up with a page that is stylistically appalling. As a rule, teach them that they must never use more than three fonts on one page, and preferably only one, though they can adjust the font size and weight (for example, using bold) as appropriate.

Task box

- What do *you* think is the most appropriate order for children to learn basic word processing techniques?
- To what extent does it depend on the age of the child?
- Make a list, and then search online for other people's suggested orders. Do you agree with them?

Using the interactive whiteboard

What follows assumes that you will find yourself teaching in a classroom with a digital projector and an interactive whiteboard (IWB) positioned so that the whole class can see it, either from their own seats or else from the carpet area in front of it.Various studies (Becta, 2004; Smith et al., 2006; Somekh et al., 2007) have indicated that although IWBs are widely used in a large proportion of classes, the extent to which they are used in a genuinely interactive way may be quite limited.

Teachers generally like IWBs, because they can prepare 'flipchart' pages beforehand, reuse them at a later stage, and present high-quality text, graphics, video and so forth in a manner they could not do with a chalk-board. All those functions, however, can be performed without the IWB, as long as you have a digital projector.

Children like IWBs. If you observe a class you can see the children snap into a more attentive mode as soon as the projected screen appears. They also like being the one selected to come to the front to write, draw or move something. This does not in itself mean that what they are doing has any particular educational validity. Getting Jimmy to stand up, wriggle his way past everyone else, pick up a word from one side of the board and move it to the other, then wriggle his way back to his place again is wasteful of time, with a minimal amount of learning taking place.

Interactive whiteboards were funded to encourage the use of interactive whole-class teaching, which had been identified (Alexander et al., 1992) as an underutilized dimension of classroom pedagogy. They were also obviously useful for the whole-class sections of the Literacy Hour and the daily mathematics lesson. There are a number of whole-class activities which can be enhanced by the use of an IWB, for example, sorting words into different groups and many more (for example, highlighting grammar features in a block of text) for which the digital projector would probably suffice. The real pedagogic skill of interactive whole-class teaching comes not in the use of flashy graphics (satisfying though these may be) but in the skilful positioning of questions and genuinely dialogic engagement in discussion on the part of the teacher. The IWB is the matrix upon which shared ideas can be worked out. We argue that it provides *a dynamic and manipulable object of joint reference which offers new forms of support for 'intersubjectivity'* (Hennessy et al., 2007).

Multimodal literacy

So far we have been discussing ways in which ICT can support or enhance the teaching of literacy. What is perhaps more significant is the way in which it can transform it, and particularly ways in which literacy itself has been redefined by advances in technology. It is no longer sufficient to think of reading entirely in terms of words on the page, that proceed from the top left to the bottom right; neither can we think of text without acknowledging the power of visual images to shape the way we receive information. As Gunther Kress (2003) amply demonstrates, literacy has shifted from being paper based to being screen based.

Most teachers are now familiar with the basic use of presentation software like Microsoft PowerPoint, and this forms a part of many lessons (and university lectures) The combination of text and graphics, particularly when ideas and images can be made to appear sequentially, is a powerful aid to the structuring of information. This is equally true for presentations constructed by children, and you should consider how this sort of software can be used as a creative writing tool.

Task box

When you have the opportunity in school, work with a group of children to create or retell a fairy story using PowerPoint.

- How many slides will you need?
- What episodes in the story go on each slide? (Hint: do not overcrowd your slide with too much text.)
- Can you find suitable illustrations to go with the text?
- Can you make different parts of the story or illustrations appear in sequence?
- Can the children work collaboratively, and reach shared decisions about how to proceed?

Similarly, the digital camera is now perhaps the most powerful aid to effective literacy teaching. We are rapidly approaching the point where everyone who has a mobile phone has an integral camera with impressive capabilities. Particularly in early years settings, children who struggle to express their ideas in writing can now capture a series of pictures which can convey meaning on their own, or around which text can be constructed. You should familiarize yourself with Microsoft Photo Story 3 (which is free to download) as a means of creating a sequence of images, to which can be added captions, voice-overs and background music. The creative possibilities held by digital storytelling have so far barely been recognized in the primary curriculum (Fox, 2007).

A few years ago it would have been unthinkable that primary children could create their own video presentations, or even their own stop-frame animations (as in, for example, 'Wallace and Gromit'). These have now been brought within the range of virtually all primary children, at a simple level through devices like the Digital Blue Movie Creator, and through the massive reductions in price of more sophisticated video cameras. Children whose lives include interaction with a number of visual media need to understand the *constructedness* of what they are watching, including the ways in which selection is made of what to portray, how camera angles influence our perception, and so forth. Many children have a quite sophisticated intuitive grasp of much of this, and the digital media now at their disposal in the classroom give them the opportunity to formulate and share that understanding.

Also, the construction of digital stories, videos and animations provides an excellent opportunity for children to practise and develop their collaboration skills. According to Mercer (1995, 2000), when working in groups children's talk might be disputational, cumulative, exploratory. Chapter 2 focuses on 'exploratory' and 'dialogic' talk in the primary classroom.

Children working together towards a clear goal, over which they have control, and for the completion of which they may have defined roles within the group, are more likely to engage in genuinely collaborative, exploratory talk.

Talking stories

For children whose reading is beginning to develop there is a wide range of 'talking stories', generally available on CD-ROM. These contain images and text, which is read aloud to the user, usually while words or phrases are highlighted. Often, clicking on single words causes them to be read individually. Some, like the Oxford Reading Tree materials, are related to existing reading scheme resources; some are spin-offs from other media, for example, featuring television characters familiar to children (for the potential value of this, see Marsh et al., 2005); many are retellings of traditional tales, and are often of fairly poor literary quality; some are a reworking of existing picture books. At their best they offer what a good picture book can offer, particularly in the *interanimation* of text and images (see, for example, Lewis, 2001), with the additional dimension that clicking on objects on the screen triggers an animation or additional dialogue. Teachers sometimes express frustration that children spend all their time clicking on animations, and little time attending to the text, but to an extent this misses the point – as in a good picture book, the 'story' is not just what is conveyed by the text (Fox, 2002). For an online version of Anthony Browne's *Voices in the Park*, in which, among other features, users can explore the events of the story via a map of the park, see Kingston University (2006).

Using the Internet

We have noted that a high proportion of primary-aged children spend a considerable amount of time using the Internet at home, sometimes using email, often playing games, sometimes completing school-related tasks, and often searching for information on subjects that interest them. What is perhaps surprising is the extent to which, according to the evidence, this takes place without any form of parental control. Every school should have an Acceptable Use Policy, to which parents and children should sign up, but you cannot patrol what children do in the privacy of their own homes. The biggest hazard to children comes from unwittingly giving out personal information to strangers in an Internet chat room. In fact, chat room use is declining, and older primary children prefer to communicate with closed groups of friends via texting or instant messaging. To be aware of the dangers, and for a common-sense view of how best to avoid them, you should familiarize yourself with the contents of the Byron Review (Byron, 2008). Your school will probably have a filter in operation to reduce the risk of access to inappropriate sites. These are sometimes over-restrictive, and deny access to harmless materials of substantial educational value. As a rule, when children are using the Internet, make sure they are aware that they are being supervised, and trust them to behave responsibly. In practice, if primary school children wander from the allotted task, it is usually for no more sinister purpose than to visit a football club or rock band website.

There is evidence that though children have technical knowledge of how to search for information using a search engine, they are not actually very good at entering the most effective search terms, or identifying which links are actually worth pursuing, so searching can take longer than necessary. It is worth spending time discussing and modelling this, as it is now a key literacy skill.

For a few years, the following bad practice has been far too common:

- The teacher sets homework – find out about Henry VIII.
- The child enters 'Henry VIII' in a search engine, and gets over 4 million 'hits'.
- The child chooses one more or less at random, prints out the web page, and hands it in – job done.

Except, of course, that the child knows nothing about Henry VIII, as the page selected was too complex for them to read or understand, so no part of the content (except perhaps the inevitable Holbein portrait) has actually passed through the child's brain.

If you find yourself in this sort of situation, think how it could be improved upon. Ask the question in such a way that the child has to conduct some more in-depth research (was Henry VIII a good musician?). Better still, set children in groups to create a presentation about Henry VIII, with each child having a particular area to investigate. Investigate the possibility of creating a webquest (see Dodge, 1995).

Blogs, wikis and email

You are probably aware of the existence of the blog (short for 'weblog'). Of the hundreds of millions of blogs that have been set up, most become entirely inactive after a short period, but some people successfully keep theirs running as a journal of their ideas, which they share with their friends. Older primary children are often expected to keep a reading journal. If your school network will permit it, why not set these up as blogs? Children with home Internet access could keep theirs up to date as a form of homework. Access to the blog can be restricted to a small group of friends, and children could 'think aloud' to each other over a period of time, perhaps as they all read the same book.

Similarly, a group could share a closed wiki. This is like a blog, but it is a page that can be added to or altered by anyone who has access to it. This would be a good way for children to engage in some shared creative writing over a period of time.

Another way is to do it by email. If children have their own email addresses, they can pass stories round a small circle of friends, each adding a paragraph or so to each story in turn. You need to decide beforehand how many passes there will be, so that children have a sense of whether they are writing the beginning, the middle or the end of the story. This idea can also work well by arranging for three or four schools to work together to pass stories on.

Podcasting

Advances in technology have meant that it is now a relatively simple matter to create a podcast. 'Podcast' is a contraction of 'iPod' and 'broadcast'. You do not need an iPod as such, but podcast files are conventionally saved as MP3 files. Children whose ideas considerably exceed their capacity to write them down can do particularly well at creating a short 'radio programme', telling their story or explaining their point of view or whatever. Podcasts can include music, or even video (technically, a 'vidcast'), and, as in several of the examples given above, are probably best when constructed by a group of children working collaboratively. Many schools now set up their own podcast 'radio stations'. Make sure that children maintain a strong sense of audience and purpose, that they think clearly about what they want to communicate and how they want to do it, and that they maintain high production values. There can be few things as boring as listening to hour after hour of children mumbling incoherently about things that nobody else is very interested in.

In conclusion

Keep in mind the point made near the beginning of this chapter – is the child controlling the computer, or is the computer controlling the child? Almost all the best ICT-based activities in literacy teaching involve the child being engaged in a creative task, very often in collaboration with others.

Concluding comments

Assuming that you are all comfortable with the title of 'digital native' and that I was charged with producing a second edition of this book in, say, two years time, what would be the new and emerging technology that I would need to suggest for inclusion in this chapter. Can you generate a list on the back of an envelope … If you are having trouble thinking up what is missing in this chapter – are you sure you can claim 'digital native' status? Do you need to ask a 10-year-old child in one of your classes?

CHAPTER 7

HANDWRITING AND TYPING

JANE MEDWELL

The illustration above shows a small, cute, 'podgy' hand holding a long thin pencil and writing. If you examine the picture carefully you can see that the writer is practising writing the alphabet. As an experienced primary and early years teacher this picture starts my mind thinking. The first set of questions I ask myself is, why has the teacher got this child practising writing letters in alphabetical order? Why would you teach a child to write capitals and lower case at the same time? Is that the best writing instrument for a beginning writer? Is this handwriting lesson linked in any way to the ongoing early reading work (perhaps, phonics instruction)? Does the photograph show that the writer is using the correct posture? Should the left hand be sitting across the page that way?

You can begin to see how complex decisions about teaching handwriting are for a teacher. In recent times teachers have been given very little direction through the Primary National Strategies on this topic. This next chapter presents what is the current 'state of the art' thinking and theorizing about the role of handwriting and typing in the Primary English classroom.

> ## This chapter includes:
>
> - handwriting or typing?
> - why is handwriting important for composing?
> - what is important in handwriting?
> - handwriting scripts, joins and fonts
> - teaching handwriting
> - what to teach in handwriting
> - teaching typing
> - posture and resources
> - assessment of handwriting and typing

Writing is a complex process which demands sophisticated orchestration of a whole range of processes. Handwriting and typing are aspects of the 'transcription' part of the models of the writing process you might have seen and, as such, might seem relatively unimportant. After all, our goal in teaching writing is for children to compose effectively. In this chapter we want to raise your awareness of the importance of handwriting and typing, and how these processes make a major contribution to children's ability to compose. This means that getting the, relatively simple, teaching of handwriting and typing right for your children can produce rich rewards in terms of children's composition and self-esteem.

Handwriting or typing?

It is tempting to believe that no one will use handwriting in the future: we will all write on computers and we will write better because of it! However, despite the huge growth in computer technology in schools, 80 per cent of American primary teachers said that children rarely used computers for writing in their classes (Cutler and Graham, 2008) and handwriting remains a daily activity for most adults, notwithstanding the availability of handheld and voice-activated devices. In theory, typing is probably a superior way to produce extended writing – it allows children to get their ideas down quickly and simply, renders writing legible very early on, reduces rewriting and effort, assists with spelling and allows for instant sharing and publication. Word processing has so much to offer the young writer that it is tempting to wonder why we teach children to write by hand at all.

One reason we use handwriting to learn to write is the convenience and nature of process itself. Unlike word processing, handwriting materials are cheap, portable and infinitely flexible. There are also clear pedagogic reasons for the use of handwriting. We teach handwriting as part of an integrated approach to literacy and we are very concerned to help children fix certain patterns in their mind: letter shapes, the correct movements for making letters, letter–sound associations, letter names for discussing spelling and patterns of letter occurrence. The actual writing of the letter shapes may help children to develop these connections, and remember them, in ways that using a keyboard does not. These two reasons suggest that handwriting is far from dead and still needs to be taught to children, alongside typing. We need to ensure that children learn handwriting and typing as early as possible. For this reason, the chapter devotes much space to the complex business of handwriting, limited space to the well-established technology of typing and none at all to input devices like voice activation and predictive text!

Why is handwriting important for composing?

Recent research into handwriting has established that handwriting is not simply a motor skill and that it does have strong effects on composing ability. Handwriting is 'language by hand' (Berninger and Graham, 1998) and involves sophisticated use of short-term working memory to mobilize the mental codes to enable individuals to write the correct letter shapes. This is a rather new way of seeing handwriting – as a mental challenge, not just a physical one, and it explains why so many children find handwriting difficult.

A key issue is how writers manage all the competing mental processes of writing at once: getting relevant ideas, knowing the requirements of the audience, shaping the writing using grammar and syntax, remembering spellings and generating the letter shapes. All these processes compete for the same, limited, short-term working memory so it is hard to manage all these things at once. The way we as adults achieve this is by making some aspects of the process, such as handwriting, automatic, so that they do not demand cognitive attention. The best analogy for this is driving a car. When you first learn to drive, every gear change, acceleration and braking movement demands thought, but an experienced driver may undertake a whole journey without paying any attention to these processes – they have become automatic. This is what we aim for in handwriting. By rendering the creation of correct letter movements (or key location) automatic, we free children from having to attend to this. However, it is far from certain when handwriting becomes automatic and there is strong evidence that for some children it continues to demand precious cognitive attention well into the secondary years. This is a serious problem because there is strong evidence that, for children whose handwriting is not automatic, the need to give attention to handwriting interferes with their ability to compose effectively (Berninger, 1994; Christensen, 2005; Jones and Christensen, 1999). This is the best reason for teaching automatic, fluent handwriting early in schooling. This issue of transcription constraining composition also applies to typing. The same children who have difficulty achieving automaticity in handwriting are likely to have difficulty in mastering automatic typing and there is no firm evidence that slow handwriters benefit from using the computer to write essays (Connelly et al., 2007). Both handwriting and typing demand explicit instruction early in schooling and the rest of this chapter addresses this issue.

What is important in handwriting?

Learning efficient, correct, early letter formation movements is the very first priority in handwriting. Sassoon (1990) wrote lyrically about the importance of learning letter shapes as movements, not just as visual patterns. The child who learns to 'cheat' to make letters look right but does not learn the correct movement cheats him or herself, because it will make joining difficult later.

The next priority in learning handwriting is automaticity. Research with 7- and 11-year-old children (Medwell et al., 2009) has shown a direct link between levels of automaticity and levels of composing. Even when general ability, age and social factors are accounted for, children whose writing is not automatic do worse at composition than those whose writing is automatic. Automaticity is not the same as neatness (it is quite possible to be neat and not automatic, and vice versa) nor is automaticity the same as copying speed. At 7 and 11, neither copying speed nor neatness affect composing significantly.

Research box

A number of studies have suggested that automaticity of letter writing is the single best predictor of length and quality of written composition in the primary years (Graham et al., 1997) and secondary school (Jones, 2004). It accounts for a large amount of the variance in composing ability. Medwell et al. (2009) investigated this proposition with 400 Year 2 and Year 11 children. They used Standard Assessment Tasks (SAT) scores for composing, and tested neatness, copying speed and automatic letter writing, using the 'alphabet test' (Berninger et al., 1991) a well-validated test which asks children to write out the alphabet in order as quickly as possible. In this way it examines how easily children can write out a sequence they know well but rarely write. Results for the Year 2 sample of 189 children established that:

- the alphabet letter test, which takes 1 minute, is a good measure of orthographic motor integration, is simple to administer to whole classes and produces useful results

- orthographic-motor integration correlated very strongly to composing quality in the Year 2 children, even when reading ability and general intelligence was taken into account
- handwriting automaticity accounted for 34 per cent of the variance in composition for the Year 2 children, with speed alone accounting for a further 10 per cent and neatness less than 2 per cent.

These findings are particularly important in the light of studies in Australia and the USA which indicate that intervention to teach key aspects of handwriting can improve not only the handwriting of target children, but also their written composition. In one study (Jones and Christensen, 1999), primary-aged children with special educational needs (SEN) which included poor levels of orthographic-motor integration experienced an eight week specialized intervention to improve their writing automaticity. This group made significant gains in composing (not just in handwriting) compared to a control group who only experienced extra writing practice (Medwell et al., 2007).

Correct movements and automaticity are the key priorities and, after these, copying speed, neatness and orientation are other factors in handwriting which children will need to learn. Another important issue is exercising judgement about when to make neatness a priority. Sassoon (1990) refers to 'having three hands' – best writing to impress, acceptable writing for efficient daily use and writing that only you will read. It is important to know when to use each hand! Handwriting is important for composing but we must also remember that handwriting is the visible trace of composition and others base their judgements (wrongly) on this. Reasonable handwriting is good for writers' self-esteem.

The teaching of handwriting has to be closely linked with the priorities discussed above. Many teaching decisions will be included in school policy, although this is often non-existent or disregarded when it comes to handwriting (Barnett et al., 2006). All schools will have made decisions about scripts, joins, tools, teaching methods and frequency of practice.

Handwriting scripts, joins and fonts

Unlike other countries, the UK does not have a prescribed handwriting style (a script and pattern of joins), so each school makes its own choice. Most choose a simple script based on a series of ovals and vertical lines which may have exit strokes (or flicks) to join letters to the next letter and entry strokes which join to the preceding letter. In England almost all children learn letter shapes which include exit and/or entry strokes from the very beginning, based on the idea that children who learn the 'stop' at the end of printed letters may have difficulty un-learning it when they move on to joining their letters.

Research box

In the 1980s and 1990s a very significant experiment took place in English schools, based on Margaret Peters's important research about spelling acquisition. This experiment involved a change in the handwriting script taught to children across Britain. Peters's research into spelling (1985; Peters and Smith, 1993) suggested that English spelling was systematic in terms not of grapho-phonemic regularity, but rather of the probability of letters occurring together, offering a high degree of visual regularity. Peters emphasized the link between visual and kinaesthetic learning of spellings, stating that 'speed of writing is clearly basic to spelling progress'. A strong theoretical case was thus made for a link between correct spelling and the use of fluent, joined-up handwriting. By learning the movements of common spelling patterns by hand (kinaesthetically) as well as by eye, it was suggested (Cripps and Cox, 1989; Peters and Smith, 1993) that writers improved their chances of producing correct spellings. The popularization of this theory in schools through spelling and handwriting schemes coincided with, or caused, a change in the handwriting of children all over the country. Handwriting schemes based on this theory advocated the use of an alphabet including exit strokes right from the beginning of writing teaching, and the joining of letters as early as possible (Cripps, 1988). There are now very few schools in England who do not use a script with exit strokes with their pupils. Alas, this major change in handwriting policy was almost totally unresearched and we have no empirical evidence about the link between handwriting and spelling!

When children have learnt most of the letter movements, they will begin to learn the joins in a prescribed pattern. This will vary depending on which joins your school has chosen. Some schools teach a fully joined script, including joining g, f, j, o, w, v, b and so on, in the hope that joined handwriting assists with correct spelling. Others choose to teach only those joins which flow 'naturally' like those between a and b but not those which demand that the writer stops the pen and then moves the other way, such as b, w, o or p. The research in this area (Sassoon, 1993) suggests that at around age 10–12 most children will adapt and personalize their own handwriting and, for the sake of speed, will drop some of the more unnatural joins. So the choice of handwriting joins may not be overwhelmingly important. In fact, many schools will base their choice on the materials or scheme they purchase to use for handwriting practice. Whichever style is chosen, this needs to be taught consistently and modelled consistently by the staff of the school.

Schools may also choose to select particular computer fonts which they think are good models to the pupils. The Sassoon font is particularly popular because of its resemblance to children's handwriting. It is also easy to read as fonts with serifs may be harder to read than the simpler sans-serif fonts. However, fonts are part of the message in writing, and selecting an appropriate font is as much part of a writing task as choosing whether to write in wax crayon or pen or which 'level' of handwriting to use. Children need to learn that although a 'smiley' font is fun, it is not appropriate for certain writing tasks. They may learn this only if given a chance to choose their own font.

Task box

School policy may not be written down. Try to identify the policy in a school you are going to work in:

- Observe what happens in your class.
- Ask a colleague about the programme.
- The handbooks and websites of any materials that are used in school are a good source of information.
- The literacy co-ordinator will be a good source of information, so arrange a time to discuss it with him or her. Review class activities and read the policies and handbooks before meeting.

Write out the alphabet script used in your school (small and capital letters). *Use it* in class.

Which letters join up? When are the different joins introduced in the school?

When is the school script used: on displays and instructions; in lessons; on handouts?

How often do your class do handwriting? When does the teacher model handwriting?

What is the usual pattern of a handwriting session in your class? (Activities, introduction, duration, and so on)

How and when is handwriting marked?

How is handwriting assessed in your school? What record is kept?

What arrangements are made for children with handwriting difficulties?

Who is left handed in your class and what arrangements are made to support them?

Teaching handwriting

Teaching early letter movements is very important and can begin when children's scribbling shows that they are using the pens, chalks etc to cross their body mid-line and are making a variety of round and more linear scribbles. Very early motor and manipulation development games (shakers, construction kits, threading etc) are great preparation for handwriting, and specific letter games like painting huge letters, tracing shapes in jelly or cornflour on trays, using big chalks outside and making letters from playdough are the beginnings of handwriting teaching. It is tempting to wonder whether the superiority of girls to boys in handwriting (Medwell et al., 2009) is related to the amount of colouring-in done before school!

Teaching any skill to the point of automaticity demands plenty of practice and this is true for both handwriting and typing. As practice may be repetitive, little and often is usually seen as superior to a single lesson per week and a short daily session of a few minutes is ideal. However, recent surveys suggest that many schools seem to find it hard to fit in any consistent handwriting teaching at all (Barnett et al., 2006). This, given the research on composing reviewed above, is a disaster! Handwriting teaching may involve use of teacher modelling on a whiteboard or electronic whiteboard and use of textbooks and cards for copying. When you do teach handwriting it needs to have some focus. You need to check children are doing correct formation and joins, or else poor habits will be learnt. Handwriting cannot just be a filler activity.

Teaching advice

Handwriting (or typing) is an area where the involvement of assistants, volunteers in school and parents at home can produce good results. Handwriting or typing demands support, reward and vigilance but little subject knowledge.

- Ensure all parents in Foundation Stage and Key Stage 1 know the letter formation each year.
- Print out or put letter formation sheets on the school website (one for left-handers and one for right-handers).
- Your handwriting scheme might have an electronic demonstration of letter formation you can add to the school website.
- If your school uses a particular typing programme, you may be able to arrange with the manufacturers for parents to buy a cut-priced version for home use. Some schools sell these to parents to let them work with their children.

- Send home worksheets or put up handwriting exercises on the school website. This could be a weekly activity for all children but it is most effective if done as a more intensive programme over a shorter time, especially if you have some children who struggle.
- Remind parents to offer plenty of praise when children do their practice.
- Take in, and praise, the work (or records of typing exercises done) children do at home. Make sure you point out improvements whenever you see them.

Parents are often very keen to supervise and reward 10 minutes of handwriting or typing practice at home each day, which can give a real boost to children's performance and self-esteem.

There is a huge range of really well planned materials available for teaching handwriting: schemes, books, interactive whiteboard programmes and computer-based typing programmes. Our latest survey shows that many schools are investing in interactive whiteboard materials. However, the same survey suggests they are not teaching handwriting very much, and often not at all! (Medwell, forthcoming). All resources are the same if they are not used. Succcssful mastery of the simple matter of handwriting and typing relies on teachers teaching handwriting and typing consistently, enthusiastically, regularly and often.

What to teach in handwriting

The first target for teaching is the letter shape movements. Achieving the correct movement is not easy and small letters are much more difficult than the capitals because they demand curved shapes and more co-ordination. This is why, when they compose something for themselves, young writers often use some capital letters – they demand much less attention to write! Many settings use line guides and abstract patterns for initial handwriting teaching, but research (Berninger, 1994) suggests that this does not transfer into effective letter writing and it is best to start with letter shape movements using large letters (paint, crayon, magic pencil, trays, and so on). At the outset it is best to worry about movements and shape, rather than size or orientation, and lines can be introduced when children have mastered most of the movement patterns.

When learning letter shape movements, many schemes start by giving children exercises which involve writing out lines of the same letters, then exercises involving writing out lines of pairs of letters and, finally, writing out sequences of words. Some of this practice is essential, but here handwriting must take a lesson from the electronic typing programmes which are so widely available. The main challenge for typing programmes is to combat the boredom of doing the repetitive practice it takes to learn typing. They do this by using short-duration activities and games, getting users to chart their progress and by setting both accuracy and speed tasks. All these techniques are relevant to handwriting.

Handwriting lessons

When you teach handwriting do not limit children's experience to copying, which is particularly difficult for some children. Handwriting lessons should include:

* some teacher modelling, especially of new joins or combinations
* some practice of specific letter movements, joins and so on. This should not just be copying but also include writing the letters in response to their names.
* some practice should be quick-fire timed activity which gets children to write something as many times as possible in a short time. This mild academic press helps develop automaticity.
* try to make handwriting fun using games like bingo to produce letters at random, or combinations of letters.

One key issue is which letters you combine to practise handwriting. Common sense, and some of the research on frequency of occurrence of letter patterns (above), suggests using commonly occurring patterns. However, if children have not developed automaticity in their handwriting, exactly the opposite may be best. Where children are struggling with automaticity it is best to do sequences of letters which would not naturally occur together. This means that each time the child writes the sequence they have to cue the mental code for the letter. The more times they do this, the more likely they are to become automatic.

Teaching typing

Typing is somewhat less demanding than handwriting, at a mental level, because accurate typing does not demand formation of shapes. Instead, keyboarding relies on the location of the correct key and, sometimes, of the keys to capitalize or perform other sophisticated functions. However, using a word processor does not improve composition when children can write faster than they can type (Connelly et al., 2007). Christensen (2004) demonstrated that the quality of the essay writing of lower secondary pupils could be improved by doing an eight-week, 20-minutes-a-day typing course. This improved their typing speed and their composition length and quality (Christensen, 2004). However, it is important that children develop and maintain automaticity in their typing, as well as their handwriting. Lewis (1998) found that children who did a six-week typing course did not show a long-term increase in typing speed and quickly reverted to the 'hunt and peck' letter location strategy. Like handwriting, typing demands intensive practice to master and longer-term practice to maintain. Reviews of the literature in the last few years suggest that touch typing (using all the fingers) is the best way to learn to type, that this should be started later in primary school and that it takes around 25–30 hours of instruction to master basic touch-typing (Freeman et al., 2005). However, this is an emerging field where practice is changing. In a world where children coming to school may have a good deal of keyboard experience, children are starting to learn to type much younger than this (Torgesen et al., 2003) and will need to begin learning before age 7 in order to achieve the UK curriculum goals (QCDA, 2010).

The good news for teaching typing is that there are many excellent programmes of activity which give children a range of games and activities which help them to develop automaticity. The bad news is that they still need to *do* these in school, regularly and often. In a crowded curriculum, with limited computer access, this may not always be the best use of time.

Posture and resources

In both handwriting and typing there are issues of posture and resources. Children learning to write and to type need to be able to sit in a stable way, with their feet on the ground. However, the needs differ. For handwriting, children need to be able to slant the paper depending on handedness. Left-handers slant the paper to the right and right-handers to the left. If a child has a hand tremor (which is very common) they may benefit from sitting almost sideways to the desk and resting the writing elbow on the desk to give greater stability, and some children will benefit from sloping writing surfaces. In typing, the priority is to sit squarely in front of the computer (not sharing) and have good hand access to keys of a reasonable size. Smaller keyboards may be useful for infants with limited digit stretch.

Around 10 per cent of the population is left-handed. Medwell et al. (2007) found that handedness was not significant in automaticity or speed of handwriting at all, as these are largely mental aspects of handwriting. There was only a very slight neatness effect which might be expected, as the English script is designed for a right hand to drag the pen across paper, not a left hand which has to push against it. Left-handers benefit from sitting on slightly higher chairs to allow them to raise their hands above the paper, and they may find it useful to hold the pencil a little further from the point, to improve visibility. There is no evidence that handedness affects typing.

Resources for teaching handwriting are often a matter of personal preference. In general, pencils are a good medium because their high graphite composition provides a good balance of 'slip' and friction for young writers. Fat, triangular pencils help children to develop a tripod grip but as long as a child does not grasp the pen in a fist, there are a surprising number of effective grips (Sassoon, 1993). Where children struggle to hold a pencil comfortably or they grip the pencil in a very tense way, it is a good idea to use a pencil grip or piece of foam held in the palm of the writing hand to relax the tension. Where children have severe motor difficulties there are large grips which offer stability but the advice of an occupational therapist should be sought. Inevitably, children want to write in a range of media, including ink. There are excellent handwriting pens available, usually with fibre tips which combine slip and friction, but viscous ballpoint ink is not a good medium – it is all slip and no friction. Fountain pens are not special, but many children think they are, and really enjoy using them.

Assessment of handwriting and typing

At present, assessment of handwriting and typing is rather ad hoc in schools (Barnett et al., 2006) and we have argued elsewhere that, nationally, we are assessing the wrong things in handwriting to promote good composition (Medwell and Wray, 2007). The statutory assessment at age 11 in England addresses only fluency judged by looking at a piece of writing and does not even seek to assess automaticity, the most important aspect of handwriting for children of that age. There is currently no statutory assessment of typing. In assessing handwriting, we believe that, in addition to the ad hoc monitoring of neatness which is already undertaken, teachers should consider the following assessment points.

At the beginning of Year 1 can the child:

- form all the letters correctly and easily when copying and in response to the letter names?
- recite and write the alphabet in correct order?

At the end of Year 2 can the child:

- form all the letters correctly and easily when copying and in response to the letter names?
- do all the joins taught up to that point easily and without obvious effort?

- write the whole alphabet from memory using correctly formed letters in alphabetical order in under 1 minute? (This is a test of automaticity.)
- locate all the alphabet keys rapidly in response to letter name or visual cues (like cards or letters on screen)?
- decide when it is appropriate to use 'neat' handwriting?

At the end of Year 6 can the child:

- copy the sentence 'The quick brown fox jumps over the lazy dog' twice, legibly, in 1 minute? (Copying speed)
- write out the alphabet in alphabetical order in legible lower and upper case letters in one minute? (Automaticity)
- decide when it is appropriate to use ordinary or 'neat' handwriting and choose an appropriate font to meet the needs of the audience for a piece of writing?
- It is impossible to give any sort of assessment of typing at this time but, ideally, we would aim for children to type as fast as they can write. This is rather ambitious at present and not an empirically based target!

If children are not able to do these things, it may be time to consider a small-group intervention to improve handwriting or even a detailed assessment of handwriting. More detailed publications such as Taylor (2001) and tests designed for school use are ideal to identify children who can benefit from additional help and to help you to target their needs (Barnett et al., 2007). Given the foregoing discussion, help with handwriting might well help with composing.

This chapter is a short introduction to some of the issues around handwriting and typing. Our national objectives for handwriting and typing are clear: children are required to form letters correctly and type accurately by age 7 and show fluency in handwriting and keyboard use by age 11. These are rightly ambitious targets because handwriting and typing constrain composition and so they are fundamental skills for children to master in order to compose successfully. Nor are handwriting and typing simply motor skills. The important aspects of handwriting are mental and can be learnt and improved. This chapter argues that handwriting and typing are worth attention precisely because they can be improved and because doing this helps children to become better composers. The research suggests that teachers do not spend much time on handwriting, are short of computer time to teach typing, and do not assess handwriting and typing or offer support for those struggling. This may be because they do not recognize the importance of handwriting and typing. With a little more attention to transcription, many children could improve their composition. This is the goal.

Concluding comments

Information about the teaching of handwriting and typing is part of the 'tool kit' that you need to be a professional and well-informed primary English teacher. You can see from reading the chapter that it is not as simple as the photograph on the front cover of this book suggests – you need to be focused, plan and reflect on how you place these lessons in your classroom, and Medwell's work in this area is fundamental to getting this right!

CHAPTER 8

AN INTRODUCTION TO ASSESSING ENGLISH

JANE MEDWELL

Assessment in English has always been a challenge and if I had a pound for every document and government policy that has been issued over the last hundred years in this country I would certainly have a fair amount of money. National Standards and the reporting of these to a range of audiences and for a range of purposes has been leading policy and practice for some years in England. Furthermore, there is an international context to the reporting of achievement and this can carry very high importance in the political arena.

More importantly, there seems to be so many acronyms and labels associated with assessment that it is sometimes difficult to get to know them all and then put them in the correct 'cognitive boxes'. Read on and you will have a very clear overview of assessment in the primary English classroom.

This chapter includes:

- the purposes of assessment
- optimizing the effectiveness of pupils' learning and teachers' teaching
- providing reliable information about national standards over time
- optimizing the learning and teaching of English through teacher assessment

  - analysing products
  - observation
  - probing and questioning

- summative and statutory assessment
- reporting to parents

In theoretical terms, assessment of children's English is perfectly simple. There are three things you can assess:

- what learners *know* (knowledge, opinions and attitudes)
- what learners *can do* (skills and processes)
- what learners *produce* (product-writing, speaking and reading).

These are our sources of data and, together, they inform the assessments we make of all aspects of English. In practice, assessment is complicated by a number of issues, including the wide range of purposes and audiences for assessments. This chapter will consider the purposes for assessing English and then look the main areas of assessment: assessment for teaching and learning and assessment for reporting. This chapter aims to improve your 'assessment literacy' (Popham, 2009) through critical discussion of approaches, rather than to offer a step-by-step guide to what is an ever-changing process.

The purposes of assessment

The Expert Group on Assessment (DCSF, 2009b) recognized four purposes for assessment:

- to optimize the effectiveness of pupils' learning and teachers' teaching
- to hold individual schools accountable for their performance
- to provide parents with information about their child's progress
- to provide reliable information about national standards over time.

All of these affect teachers, but some affect teaching more directly than others. We shall discuss and consider who might have an interest in each of these purposes.

Optimizing the effectiveness of pupils' learning and teachers' teaching

To make the most of pupil learning in English we need to measure progress. Assessment measures progress in English against a range of criteria. In England the criteria for the Early Years Foundation Stage (EYFS) are related to the Communication Language and Learning (CLL) assessment scales:

- language for communication and thinking
- linking sounds and letters
- reading
- writing.

Each of these has 9 levels.

In Key Stages 1 and 2 the criteria are related to one of the four statements of attainment for English:

- EN1 Speaking and Listening
- EN2 Reading
- EN3 Writing.

as well as languages Statement of Attainment (SoA).

Each of these attainment targets sets out national standards of performance – what children should know, understand and be able to do – in English at nine levels. There are sub-levels for the first three levels and p-scales for children with special needs who are working below level 1.

These national criteria allow children, parents and teachers to judge performance and measure the progress of children of similar ages across the primary phase. Where assessment contributes to planning, it is called *formative* assessment. As a result of this, teachers pinpoint class targets and individual targets for children.

Schools also administer a periodic *summative*, or 'snapshot', assessment to their children using teacher assessment, statutory tests and tasks. They report these assessment results to government and parents and record the results in such a way that indicates whether children have made progress over a longer period.

To optimize learning and teaching, teachers aim to make teaching address the learning needs of the children as closely possible. Sometimes teachers use assessment to identify particular difficulties in English that individual children may have, so they can focus teaching on these areas. This can be done at several levels and there is a statutory procedure for diagnosing the difficulties faced by children with special educational needs. However, as a teacher you will need to be able to make a diagnostic assessment of children's phonics knowledge, mark written work diagnostically and use processes such as running record, a technique which is very useful for inferring the reading strategies used by a beginner reader.

As a result of formative assessment of children's progress, or diagnosing children's difficulties, teachers make judgements about the kinds of differentiation, materials and teaching methods that best fit individual children's needs so that teaching can be tailored to these needs. In this way assessment feeds into planning. This purpose for assessment is the reason the term *Assessment for Learning* makes so much sense to teachers.

Assessments of pupil progress will also contribute to evaluation of the teaching methods and materials experienced by the children, in order to optimize teaching and learning. The extent of children's learning is not the only criterion for evaluating a new teaching approach, but assessment of pupil achievement is an important and necessary criterion for judging the success of innovation. Evaluation of methods and materials will take place at both a local and a national level. For instance, a school governing body or senior management team might look at the statutory assessment results of its schools over a number of years to evaluate the impact of electronic whiteboards in school. Nationally, the statutory assessment results are one of the factors against which the success of initiatives such as *Letters and Sounds* or *Assessment of Pupil Progress* will be measured. Ultimately, approaches and initiatives are designed to optimize children's learning and teachers' teaching, and they must be judged on whether they achieve this goal.

Providing reliable information about national standards over time

Rigorous, comparable assessments allow us to know whether national standards have been maintained and improved. Comparisons such as the Progress in International Reading Literacy Study (PIRLS) (Mullis et al., 2008) and the Programme for International Student Assessment, or PISA (OECD, 2000), allow us to compare achievement in literacy in different countries and the 'headline' results of such studies are often used as a clarion call for change by politicians (Baker, 2005). Similar nationwide data, based on nationally agreed criteria such as the National Curriculum level descriptors, is also important at a national and whole-school level. The assessments used for this sort of measurement are the results of statutory assessment of English at the end of EYFS Key Stage 1 and Key Stage 2. When compared with data either from a 'baseline' measure of children at entry level or with the results of the previous key stage a measure of 'value added' – the amount of performance increase between assessments – can be made. In response to this information the government (or local authority or school) sets targets for aspects of teaching it wishes to improve. Ultimately, these targets are addressed by each school, key stage and class within a school and affect the work of each teacher.

Assessments are also used to compare pupils within the national sample, within smaller groups such as such social, gender or race groups. These comparisons can reveal which groups of pupils are making the best progress and which groups are underperforming. For example, it is regularly noted that a national comparison of pupils in writing reveals that boys are under-performing (Bearne and Warrington, 2003); that is, they perform less well than girls at the same ages. This has led to a national effort to improve boys' writing (National Strategies/DCSF, 2008).

Holding individual schools accountable for their performance

Comparisons can also be made within areas, schools and classes, to reveal whether national issues apply in a particular class or school. Such comparisons may be used as a means of allocating resources to particular groups. A school or a local authority may, for example, decide to provide extra teaching equipment or teaching help to a group of children who have been identified as having special needs. At the moment, one-to-one tuition is being offered to children who are not making adequate progress when compared with their peers (TDA, 2009). Naturally, the progress made by children will be used to evaluate how effectively resources are used by each school.

Comparison between schools on the basis of Statutory Assessment results will inform Office for Standards in Education (Ofsted) inspections into how well the school is achieving. The results will be made available (and published in local newspapers) to inform parents and will be scrutinized by local authorities to pinpoint support needs. This comparison between schools is not a simple matter because school intakes and circumstances differ enormously, and useful comparisons try to take these factors into account. To do this, school performances are compared with 'benchmarks' of groups of schools judged to be generally similar in circumstances and intake.

Optimizing the learning and teaching of English through teacher assessment

The measurement of progress is the main focus of *formative* assessment, that is, assessment which is actually used to adapt teaching to meet the needs of the learners. This term has been criticized as being simply another way of saying that assessment is carried out frequently and is planned at the same time as teaching (Assessment Reform Group, 2006) so you will see the term *Assessment for Learning* (AfL) used. This term has an additional power and resonance for teachers because it promotes a powerful focus on learning and this is what formative assessment (AfL) is about.

To return to the sources of data identified at the very start of this chapter, teacher assessment is based upon:

- analysing what children actually produce – this involves looking at writing, analysing, reading aloud, behaviour in one-to-one, group or shared reading, analysing what children say
- what children actually do – observing writing processes, reading processes and speaking and listening processes
- what children know – asking children what they know, their opinions and attitudes.

By making these assessments as part of the planning and teaching cycle, teachers can address the five key factors identified by Black and Wiliam (below) which promote assessment which really improves learning.

Research box

Professors Paul Black and Dylan Wiliam synthesized evidence from over 250 studies linking assessment and learning (1998). The outcome was a clear and incontrovertible message: that initiatives designed to enhance effectiveness of the way assessment is used in the classroom to promote learning can raise pupil achievement. The research indicates that improving learning through assessment depends on five, deceptively simple, key factors:

- the provision of effective feedback to pupils
- the active involvement of pupils in their own learning
- adjusting teaching to take account of the results of assessment
- a recognition of the profound influence assessment has on the motivation and self-esteem of pupils, both of which are crucial influences on learning
- the need for pupils to be able to assess themselves and understand how to improve.

At the same time, several inhibiting factors were identified:

- a tendency for teachers to assess quantity of work and presentation rather than the quality of learning

- greater attention given to marking and grading, much of it tending to lower the self-esteem of pupils, rather than providing advice for improvement
- a strong emphasis on comparing pupils with each other which demoralizes the less successful learners
- teachers' feedback to pupils often serves social and managerial purposes rather than helping them to learn more effectively
- teachers not knowing enough about their pupils' learning needs.

These findings have been exceptionally influential on policy and underpin the development of Assessment of Pupil Progress (QCA, 2008).

Assessment of Pupil Progress (APP) is a structured approach to teacher assessment which helps teachers to make judgements on pupils' progress. This approach uses observation, diagnostic analysis of children's products and discussion to help teachers fine-tune their understanding of learners' needs and to tailor their planning and teaching accordingly, by enabling them to

- track pupils' progress
- use diagnostic information about pupils' strengths and weaknesses to improve teaching, learning and pupils' progress
- make reliable judgements related to national standards drawing on a wide range of evidence.

Assessment of Pupil Progress involves teachers using charts of statements for each level and sub-level of reading, writing, speaking and listening, to make a detailed assessment of a small number of children in their classes. Teachers use these charts to record the evidence of children's performance and ensure teachers really know what performance at each sub-level or level 'looks like'. The teachers are then able to review the evidence for the other children and assign a level or sub-level to each child's performance.

A key issue in all assessment, including teacher assessment, is to ensure that the inferences drawn from the evidence are valid and reliable. A *valid* assessment is one which measures what it is intended to measure. So, for instance, assessing the quality of a child's written composition by counting the number of words written would not be valid because composition is not simply about length. This is why we have nationally agreed level descriptors for each Statements of Attainment (SoA) and why schemes like APP demand a wide range of evidence for performance at each level.

A *reliable* assessment is one which consistently achieves the same results with the same (or similar) cohort of students. This is why teachers undertake so much moderation. By assessing pieces of children's activity together (written scripts, videos of talk, podcasts, and so on) teachers can establish shared and consistent understandings about levels and how they assess them. The training standards files are materials supplied for APP which exemplify the standards and allow teachers to practice making reliable judgements.

Analysing products

A great deal can be gleaned from analyses of the language and literacy children produce, including readings to an adult, recordings, writing and speaking in groups, pairs and as podcasts and recordings. By assessing what children *can* do, we can identify what it is that they still need to learn to do

Error analysis is based upon the theory that the mistakes a child makes when reading aloud from a text betray a great deal about how that child is tackling the reading task. As an example, the following sentence in a reading book, 'The man got on his horse' was read by a child as, 'The man got on his house'. Because the word 'house' does not make sense in this context, it is fairly safe to assume that making sense was not the chief preoccupation of this child, who seems rather to be attending to the initial letters of the word. Another child read the sentence as, 'The man got on his pony'. This child seems to have been attending more to the meaning, even to the extent of ignoring what the word looked like. These two children seem to have different approaches to the task of reading, which lead them to 'miscue' in different ways.

Research box

American researchers, the Goodmans, were responsible for much of the important work related to error analysis (see Goodman et al., 1987, for a full account of miscue analysis). Clay (1979) has looked at the reading of younger children and developed a procedure called running record, which is part of the reading recovery programme for early intervention and has been included in the Key Stage1 Standard Assessment Tasks for a number of years.

The misreading of one word is not sufficient evidence upon which to base a complete assessment. The technique of miscue analysis or running record, therefore, uses a child's oral reading of much longer texts and tries to point out patterns in the kinds of misreadings that the child produces. It is usually carried out with the child reading from his or her normal book, and the teacher recording exactly what the child reads on another copy of the text. There are several suggested coding systems for this recording, although the exigencies of time usually mean that the simplest possible system is most effective (it is also possible to tape-record the child's reading for later more detailed analysis, if this is required). The child may then be asked to retell the story just read, so as to provide an indication of comprehension. The miscues the child has made are then analysed by the teacher for patterns, which may indicate particular features of the child's approach to reading.

Following the reading both running record and miscue analysis should be followed by a discussion about the text, so that the child's comprehension can be estimated and evaluated. This technique, in common with all assessment techniques, is never the sole source of information available to the teacher but it is a very diagnostic examination of a reading and is a really useful approach to use with any child who is struggling.

Task box

Looking diagnostically at errors is a very important skill for you. By doing a miscue analysis you will change the way you listen to readers. You should do a miscue analysis or running record with four or five children. Use the code in the Statutory Reading Task for Key Stage1 Teacher Handbook.

Select a passage as part of a book. Make sure it is a little difficult for the child. Select a child to read with you and tell them you would like them to read but that you will not help them. The child should do what he or she normally does if he or she gets to a difficult bit.

- Read the text up to the passage you have selected.
- Ask the child to read your selected passage and mark errors using the code above.
- Read the rest of the story to the child.
- Ask the child to retell the passage and discuss it.
- Analyse the miscues and comprehension as shown in the discussion.

Analysis of written products

Teachers mark and assess a great deal of writing and it cannot all be marked at the same level. When marking any work, the teacher refers to the objectives for that work and the assessment criteria which are either implied by the objective or which have been specifically stated. The marking may be evidence for a wider assessment scheme such as APP. The aims originally formulated for this piece of work are fundamental to the marking and assessment value of the work, which is why assessment is a cyclical process. The results of one assessment feed into the criteria you set for the next. The assessment must also take into consideration the capabilities of the children producing the work. A piece of writing may be good for one child, but well below another's capacity. The assessment should also focus on the intended audience for the writing, and whether it is appropriate for this audience.

Each school will have a policy which offers teachers guidance for marking and, possibly, a prompt sheet for use when thoroughly marking a piece of children's writing. This sort of piece may well be stored in a portfolio of evidence for later review of progress or reporting teacher assessment at the end of year, but the results should always be shared with the author first.

Teaching activity

This schema for assessing writing, Key Stage 1, is adapted from the Qualifications and Curriculum Development Agency (QCDA) at http:// curriculum.qcda.gov.uk/uploads/English%201999%20programme%20 of%20study_tcm8-12054_tcm8-16038.pdf By using it with some pieces of children's writing you can begin to develop your experience at applying criteria to work.

NAME:

DATE:

CONTEXT OF WRITING:

What is your overall assessment of this piece of writing?

CONTENT		**Score**
Level 1	Do the words and phrases communicate meaning?	1 2
Level 2	Does the narrative make sense to the reader?	3 4
Level 3	Is the writing in the correct form, clear and/or imaginative?	5 6
Level 4	Are the ideas sustained and appropriately organised using effective vocabulary?	7 8

GRAMMAR and PUNCTUATION		**Score**
Level 1	Are full stops either in their writing or read by the child?	1 2 3
Level 2	Are ideas sequenced, with some sentences having capital letters and full stops?	4 5 6
Level 3	Are the ideas extended sequentially, with full stops, capital letters and question marks usually used correctly?	7 8 9
Level 4	Are simple sentences correctly punctuated, with some correct punctuation in complex sentences?	10 11 12

SPELLING		**Score**
Level 1	Has there been independent use of sound–symbol relationships and phonological patterns to spell common words?	1 2
Level 2	Are the majority of monosyllabic words spelt correctly or phonetically plausible?	3 4
Level 3	Is the spelling, including common polysyllabic words (for example national literacy strategy list year 4) usually accurate?	5 6
Level 4	Is the spelling, including regular polysyllabic words, generally accurate?	7 8

PRESENTATION		**Score**
Level 1	Are the letters clearly shaped and correctly orientated?	1
Level 2	Are the letters accurately formed and consistent in size?	2
Level 3	Is the handwriting correctly joined and legible?	3
Level 4	Does the presentation include fluently joined handwriting?	4

Score to level

Score in range	< 4	4–8	9–18	19–27	28–32
Level	W	1	2	3	4

Observation

Teachers observe children working all the time. As a result of this observation they make assessments of children's abilities and attitudes, and plan future work. But it is the poor relation of assessment techniques because teachers may not feel they are 'doing' enough when they are observing. Yet observation has a great deal of potential. Its greatest strength lies in the fact that it enables assessments to be made while children are actually engaged in language work, and does not require them to be withdrawn from it into a special testing situation. It therefore enables direct analysis of the child's process of working, without which assessment must be incomplete.

To use observation deliberately as an assessment technique requires a systematic approach. It also requires some means of recording the information gained rather than relying on memory alone.

A systematic approach will involve first of all knowing exactly what one is going to be looking for. This might mean listing the skills it is hoped to assess, and preparing a checklist of them. An alternative approach to structuring observation is to list the activities the children will be doing, and leaving space for noted observations about their performance. In either case, your priority will be to ensure you sample the types of talk for each child you need to make judgements about performance.

Observation can be guided by a list of points to look for, suggestions for which will come from the progress criteria you are using. It is important to state that these points are not intended to be simply 'ticked off' as assessments are made. They ideally require a more qualitative response, which can be added to as more information is acquired and, of course, revised as progress is made. At the very least, these points need to be noted with a record of the evidence. The APP assessment guidelines offer examples of the behaviours you might observe. The evidence for this might be noted down from an individual or group reading session.

Probing and questioning

To find out what children think and know as they read, write and discuss you may want to conduct discussions as part of reading, writing and discussion tasks or have regular, conferences with individual children about their literacy. Three types of probing questions are useful in this.

1. Looking-back questions

These are of the type, 'Can you tell me how you did that?' They can be useful when looking at children's work alongside them. The children's answers to this question may well reveal a great deal about their perceptions of the processes of language. The following extract from a conversation between a teacher and 7-year-old Feema is an example of this approach. Feema has just written her version of the story of Red Riding Hood in which the heroine is menaced by an alien rather than a wolf.

Teacher: Oh, that's an interesting story, Feema! Where did you get the idea from?
Feema: From my book. We don't have wolves here any more.
T: Yes, that's right. Can you tell me how you started writing your story? What did you do first?
F: Me and Joanne talked about it and … we just wrote it.
T: Did you write it together?
F: Well … at first we wrote the same thing … then Joanne wanted to change hers and I didn't. So we wrote different ones.
T: Did you change your story at all? As you were writing it?
F: I changed some words … Emma told me how to spell them.
T: Oh, Emma helped you too? What did she do?
F: She read the story after I finished it. She told me my spellings.
T: Yes … Now, did you plan to do anything with your story when you finished it? … Who did you want to read it?
F: Put it on the wall?

As a result of this conversation the teacher was able to make several observations about this child's approach to and expertise in language processes. Feema had clearly been able to extract information from a book and use it in another context: a fairly advanced skill for a 7-year-old. She had been able to participate in discussion both in planning her writing and in editing it. She was prepared to work on her writing collaboratively although this did not survive the disagreement with her partner. Her approach to the writing process showed some evidence of planning although this was not extensive. She was unclear about the destination and audience for her writing and saw revision purely in terms of editing spellings.

All these evaluations would require further investigation, but it is clear from this brief extract what a wealth of information the teacher was able to glean simply by asking questions that caused Feema to reflect on what she had done.

2. Looking-forward questions

An alternative kind of question can be of the type, 'Can you tell me how you will do that?' They ask children to think about their actions before they do them. It is, of course, possible that because they are made by the question to think through in advance what they will do, they actually perform differently than they would have done without the question. The question may therefore have a teaching role, as well as being a way of seeing whether they know what to do.

Questions such as the following are of this type:

- When you go to the library to look for that book, can you tell me what you will do?
- Now, you are going to write your report on sports day for the school newspaper. How will you start?
- This group are going to discuss your puppet play. How are you going to make sure everyone gets a fair chance to say what they think?

As a result of questions like these the teacher is able both to make an initial assessment of children's approaches to the process, and to prompt them in a way that may actually develop their thinking.

3. Thinking-out-loud questions

These are of the type, 'What are you thinking as you are doing that?' They can help make children's thinking about certain tasks explicit and alert the teacher to faulty approaches. They may include questions like:

- As you make notes from that book, can you tell me why you are choosing those things?
- How did you know that word said 'unusual'?

- How can you work out what might come next?
- Now, is your discussion going well? Have you found any problems?

It is quite likely that, in general, teachers ask too few questions like this. In addition to providing useful information about the way children are thinking, they can have the important effect of heightening children's awareness of the way they are using language. Developing this 'metalinguistic awareness' is an important task for the teacher of language and literacy.

Summative and statutory assessment

Summative assessment, also called Assessment of Learning (AoL), is the sort of assessment which takes a 'snapshot' of what the child can do in each area so that performance can be reported to parents, government and, of course, to the child. This has to be done, statutorily, at the end of the EYFS for all children in settings and at the end of Key Stages 1 and 2 for children in state maintained schools.

Statutory assessment at the end of EYFS

The EYFS profile is a way of summarizing each child's development and learning attainment at the end of the EYFS. The EYFS profile must be completed in the final term of the academic year in which the child reaches the age of five. For most children, this is at the end of the reception year (Year R) in primary school.

The EYFS profile is based on practitioners' ongoing observations and assessments, and each child's level of development should be recorded against the four CLL assessment scales.

Statutory assessment at the end of Key Stage1 and Key Stage 2

The level descriptions in the National Curriculum are the basis for judging children's levels of attainment at the end of the key stage. Level descriptions indicate the type and range of performance that children working at a particular level should characteristically demonstrate. Teachers should use their knowledge of a child's work to judge which level description best fits that child's performance across a range of contexts. The aim is for a rounded judgement which:

- is based on knowledge of how the child performs over time across a range of contexts
- takes into account strengths and weaknesses of the child's performance
- is checked against adjacent level descriptions to ensure that the level awarded is the closest match to the child's performance in each attainment target.

Teachers are required to summarize their teacher assessments at the end of the key stage for each eligible child, in the form of:

- a level for *each attainment target* in English
- an *overall subject level* which is calculated by aggregating the teacher assessment attainment target levels.

The use of P scales is statutory for pupils with special educational needs who are working below level 1 of the National Curriculum and schools use P scales to record and report the achievements of those children in English.

At both key stages speaking and listening is only assessed through teacher assessment but at Key Stage 1 teachers are required to choose either the standard assessment test or standard assessment task for each child and use this to inform their judgement. For reading and writing, where teachers reach a level 2 judgement, they should then consider whether the performance is just into level 2, securely at level 2 or at the top end of level 2. This refines the judgement into 2C, 2B or 2A.

Key Stage 2 grades for all three attainment targets are reported to government and parents. For Speaking and Listening (AT1) this is based entirely on teacher assessment. However, for reading and writing there are statutory tests which all eligible children must undertake, with separate assessments of reading, writing and spelling. The Key Stage 2 tasks and tests are, at the moment, a national examination, administered on a set timetable under given conditions so that the results can be considered valid and reliable. They are marked by markers outside the schools and the results are sent to schools by the end of term. At the moment, single-level tests are being piloted and science is being assessed through sampling the population, so change may be afoot.

The biggest impact of this testing is that, as a teacher, you have a responsibility to prepare children for the tests. In assessment terms, 'testwiseness' (Flippo, 2005) may be as important as the ability being assessed in getting good results. If children in other classes have been prepared for the format of the examination and yours have not, they will be at a disadvantage.

Reporting to parents

This chapter is a brief introduction to assessment of English, but the importance of reporting to parents cannot be ignored. The school has a statutory duty to report to parents and to give them the opportunity to discuss the report of their child's progress. Schools take this very seriously, as do parents. In seeking experience to prepare for a teaching post, observing a parents' evening and writing some reports with the support of an experienced teacher are indispensible experiences.

For children in Year 1 and above you should report briefly on achievements in English and other activities, highlighting development needs. For children at the end of Key Stage 1 you should also report the teacher assessment levels with a brief commentary setting out what these show about the child's progress in English in relation to other children in the same year, drawing attention to any particular strengths and weaknesses.

The information for parents at Key Stage 2 is similar, and at the end of the key stage must include the results of any National Curriculum tests taken during the year, by level, with comparative data about the children's performance in that year group within the school and across the country.

Conclusion

This chapter is a short introduction to some key issues in assessment. Planning and assessment are the key to effective English teaching but there is no one correct way to assess learners' English performance. This is because the range of purposes for assessment address the needs of vastly different audiences and the simple numerical data which might suit government needs will not serve the teacher well in planning for the progress of the individual or group. All the purposes for assessment eventually affect teachers, because it is teachers who are responsible for addressing the targets set for the nation, particular groups, schools and individuals.

For teachers, the real key to effective assessment of English is managing and recording the three basic approaches to assessment: analysing products, observing processes and questioning. The best way to achieve this will depend on your class and support. In addition to the AfL teachers need for teaching, AoL (summative) assessment places additional demands on the teacher in terms of preparation of children for tests and management of the processes. These processes will change annually and you need to be fully aware of the statutory aspects of assessment and reporting to parents.

Concluding comments

This is the beginning of your journey in learning about using assessment in the primary English classroom as the pivot point for your planning, and teaching. Medwell has provided us with a comprehensive introduction to the area and linked assessment to planning, teaching and thinking about children's learning.

CHAPTER 9

PLANNING FOR LANGUAGE LEARNING AND TEACHING IN PRIMARY SCHOOL

CARRIE ANSELL

Now, it is time to bring the knowledge that you have gained and been introduced to in the last eight chapters together. Planning for teaching is a fundamental tool for the teacher and, with the centrality of the teaching of English in the primary classroom, a thoughtful and well-informed approach to this is essential.

The special delight with this chapter is the close focus on planning for diversity in the primary English classroom and that it provides access to further resources. Diversity in the English classroom requires an inclusive curriculum and this chapter provides ideas for thinking about inclusion at the centre of the planning process rather than as an 'add-on'.

> **This chapter includes:**
>
> - core principles of planning for language and literacy learning
> - planning inclusive language and literacy learning
> - a framework for planning for all learners
> - using children's texts as a starting point for planning in literacy
> - cross-curricular planning in language and literacy
> - planning communication, language and literacy in the Early Years Foundation Stage (EYFS)
> - bringing all the elements together: planning an effective literacy lesson.

If you want to be an outstanding teacher of English in the primary school you will need to bring all the subject and pedagogical knowledge that you have acquired and all your enthusiasm for teaching English together in the planning process. Essentially, planning effective English lessons means making sure that you cater for the learning needs of the whole range of learners in your classroom and beyond. Some of the questions which come to mind might be: how do we effectively plan for English teaching and learning in schools today? What are the core principles of teaching communication, language and literacy that inform the planning process? How do the four main strands of literacy – speaking, listening, reading and writing – interrelate? What does medium- and short-term planning in language and literacy look like, in both the primary and Foundation Stage curriculum? What kind of planning will be inclusive for bilingual learners and pupils who are in the early stages of learning English?

This chapter considers the core principles that underpin language and literacy planning. By thinking closely about planning for all learners, we are able to really think about what language demands are made on learners in the English classroom and focus on providing an inclusive curriculum. Mindful of its key principle – that planning for inclusion threads throughout and informs all planning – this chapter will also focus on planning for bilingual learners and encompass an important focus on theoretical aspects of bilingualism. In particular, it will reflect critically on the role that interdependence theory (Cummins and Swain, 1986) has in planning language and literacy lessons for bilingual learners.

Core principles of planning for language and literacy learning

The key to effective planning in language and literacy is to be aware of recognized core principles which relate to an understanding of how children learn from a sociocultural perspective (Bruner, 1976). Language and literacy learning is essentially built on a desire to communicate. Literacy has its beginnings in social relationships with significant others and the need to make meaning is at the heart of these relationships.

- Speaking and listening is a core communicative skill, but is also the foundation of language and literacy development.
- Listening to and making narratives with stories and characters is crucial for vocabulary and language comprehension development in young children.
- Language and literacy learning takes place in multi-sensory and 'language rich' environments. In the Early Years Foundation Stage, an 'enabling environment' is defined as one which supports children's language learning through planned experiences that are challenging, but achievable.
- All children bring with them existing language and literacy knowledge and skills that they draw upon. Children will have internalized stories and children's literature that they have heard in their first or additional language, and these conventions may appear in their own speech or writing.
- Early Years Foundation Stage practitioners place great emphasis on play in planning for communication, language and literacy. Tina Bruce in her book on the essentials of literacy (Bruce, 2009) describes 12 features of children's 'free flow' play. Children, through their play, will create narratives based on stories and characters they have heard from favourite books that have been read to them or that they have listened to on DVD.
- Children live in 'simultaneous worlds' (Kenner, 2004). They transform the languages and cultures they use to create new forms relevant to the purpose needed (Gregory et al., 2004).
- Modelling is an essential part of learning new vocabulary, grammatical structures and discourse in language and literacy learning. Adults or peers, often bilingual, can be models in this interactive process and 'scaffold' language and literacy learning.
- Using appropriate, engaging and inspiring children's texts as a starting point for planning is crucial. If children enjoy language and literacy learning, then they will be more likely to be motivated to become lifelong readers and writers.

Planning inclusive language and literacy learning

Schools have a responsibility to provide a broad and balanced curriculum for all pupils. The National Curriculum is the starting point for planning a school curriculum that meets the specific needs of individuals and groups of individuals, (DfEE/QCA, 2000: 30)

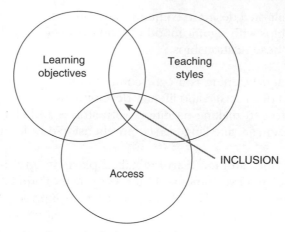

Figure 9.1   Planning for an inclusive curriculum

The National Curriculum inclusion statement (DfEE/QCA, 2000) sets out three circles of inclusion which will inform your planning for language and literacy learning and ensure participation and equality of opportunity. These circles are set out in the form of a Venn diagram (Figure 9.1), signalling that all three elements are interlinked and need to be addressed in planning and teaching.

This statement suggests that the way to ensure that planning is inclusive is by considering the three core planning areas. Setting suitable learning objectives and challenges, considering teaching and learning styles, providing support which ensures equal access to the curriculum and responding to pupil's diverse needs will produce a central core of curriculum planning which will be inclusive.

A framework for planning for all learners

Medium- and short-term planning in language and literacy

Medium-term planning in literacy usually takes place over several weeks. In the Primary Framework for Literacy (DfES, 2006b) this is generally referred to as a series of units of work, also known as a scheme of work. The units of work in the Primary Framework for Literacy break down into blocks of narrative, poetry and non-fiction. Each unit contains an outline of literacy objectives and word level skills such as phonics, spelling and handwriting. Many teachers find these useful and build them into their planning, although in order for the curriculum you are teaching to be relevant and creative, children's interests and linguistic and cultural backgrounds need to be taken into account. An example of a unit of work for literacy in Year 3 can be seen in Table 9.1.

Table 9.1 Year 3 units of work

Narrative, plays and scripts (18 weeks)	Unit 1 Stories with familiar settings (3 weeks)	Unit 2 Myths and legends (4 weeks)	Unit 3 Adventure and mystery (4 weeks)	Unit 4 Authors and letters (3 weeks)	Unit 5 Dialogue and plays (4 weeks)
Non-fiction (11–12 weeks)	Unit 1 Reports (4 weeks)	Unit 2 Instructions (3–4 weeks)	Unit 3 Information texts (4 weeks)		
Poetry (5 weeks)	Unit 1 Poems to perform (1 week)	Unit 2 Shape poetry and calligrams (2 weeks)	Unit 3 Language play (3 weeks)		

Source: DfES (2006b)

When planning using a scheme of work such as this, you will want to also consider:

- your children – the languages they speak, their cultural background, whether they have additional special educational needs, if they are highly proficient in a particular area of learning, their previous learning and out of school learning
- resources that you will need; especially children's texts which will engage, stimulate and involve children
- language and literacy objectives which will link to the National Curriculum Programme of Study
- ways in which you might assess children's language and literacy learning in order to inform your planning further.

Short-term planning is usually the equivalent of a weekly plan, or can take place over a series of individual lessons. Practitioners will plan their learning intentions for the activities, including differentiation for all learners and appropriate resources for any anticipated shared, guided and independent work.

Integrating speaking, listening, reading and writing

The importance of planning speaking and listening tasks as the foundation for language and literacy learning cannot be underestimated. All children learn to speak first when learning a language. For all learners, language lies at the heart of a person's culture and identity. We have already found out that bilingual learners use languages for different purposes. Fluid language use is the norm, with learners moving between and across languages (Conteh et al., 2007). Fluent bilingual learners have the facility to 'code-switch' between two or more languages more than other bilingual learners. A new-to-English bilingual learner will benefit from being able to express ideas in their first language and English before embarking on a task involving reading and writing. This is best done in collaborative group work, ideally with a speaker of the same language. It is important to bear in mind though, that not all bilingual learners will be literate in their first language and some languages are only oral in nature.

An understanding of the core relationship between speaking, listening, reading and writing will, in fact, form the basis of all planning in literacy. Speaking and listening should be planned during all phases of the teaching sequence – when teaching reading and familiarizing children with language features of texts, teaching reading strategies and getting children to respond to texts, and when teaching writing – stimulating writing, discussing audience and purpose and when planning, designing and editing writing. In its guidance on planning in literacy, the Primary National Strategy has provided some case studies of teachers who have planned using 'talk for writing' resources and ideas. The planning and teaching sequence has encapsulated the importance of talk or 'capturing ideas' in Figure 9.2.

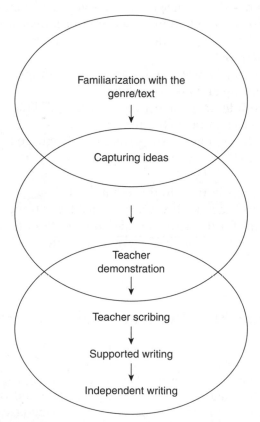

Figure 9.2 Integrated unit for literacy: teaching process
Source: Adapted from the Primary National Strategy (2006b)

Furthermore, the National Strategy is also now using the term, 'book talk' to describe children's extended opportunities to respond and engage with texts. This approach has a three-part process:

1 Eliciting response (Tell me what you thought/felt about ...)
2 Extending response (Tell me more about ...)
3 Encouraging critique (Do you agree with ... ?)

All three steps are supposed to generate 'rich dialogue'. However, Robin Alexander (2008) argues that it is vital that a shift in classroom culture is needed to allow for 'dialogic teaching'. In an environment in which there is dialogic teaching, the learning is about the teacher and the learner engaged in purposeful and reciprocal talk. According to Alexander, such talk is:

- *collective,* with teachers and learners learning together
- *reciprocal*, where teachers and learners can share ideas
- *supportive,* with children helping each other and articulating ideas freely
- *cumulative*, with teachers and children building on each other's ideas
- *purposeful,* where teachers have planned with specific learning objectives in mind.

When planning for language and literacy it is important to consider ways in which you will nurture a classroom culture in which children feel valued and able to freely express their thoughts, ideas and opinions. Planning for dialogic talk means structuring lessons in order to stimulate and extend children's thinking and learning further.

Using children's texts as a starting point for planning in literacy

The most important factor that creates a literate classroom is a literate teacher (Goodwin, 2006). The research from the Barrs and Cork project, *The Reader in the Writer* (2001), realized the relationship between reading quality texts and children's achievement in writing. Children need time to talk about books, interpret what they have read and design texts for themselves. Indeed, *interpreting* literacy is arguably far more enriching and motivating for children than an emphasis on planning to teach the 'mechanics' of literacy. Over-analysing texts and dissecting them may spoil the enjoyment and quality of children's response to them. Therefore a balanced approach should always be sought.

Selecting the text appropriate for your children can be more of a challenge if you are not a reader of children's books. If this is the case, then do not despair – it is never too late to begin. Children's books are enjoyable to read and most importantly, quicker to read than adult books! Help is also at hand from valued sources, such as the Centre for Language in Primary Education (CLPE) Core Book List 2008, which is a comprehensive list of children's texts developed with classroom teachers. That, along with other resources, including the CLPE BookPower project which is supported by learning aims and teaching approaches and resources, informed the Power of Reading project which began in 2004 and is now entering its fifth year in 2009. This project aimed to enhance both teachers and children's pleasure in reading and raise achievement in children's literacy. These are available at http://www.clpe.co.uk/publications. There are also a number of useful websites which review children's texts and link them to planning in literacy. For instance, the Devon County Council literacy planning site has a useful resource called Texts that Teach, downloadable at http://www.des-education.org. This has helpfully linked some children's texts to the Primary National Strategy Framework for Literacy learning objectives.

It is crucial to understand that texts can be electronic as well as paper based. Using film, visual images and media texts, particularly those which tap into children's popular culture (Marsh and Millard, 2000) should not be neglected. Many children are engaging with a range of modes in literacy at home and are developing new skills and ways of interacting with them which, as teachers, you can exploit.

Cross-curricular planning in language and literacy

Planning cross-curricular links in language and literacy learning is important so that:

- children can practice and apply their learning in a different context
- as a teacher, you can see the gaps in their understanding and linguistic ability
- children can see that literacy can also be learnt in meaningful and authentic contexts
- the language of the subject is reinforced, using the literacy skills that the children have acquired, which in turn enhances the learning of the subject itself

The *Independent Review of the Primary Curriculum: Final Report* by Jim Rose (2009) suggests organization of the curriculum from September 2011 into six areas of learning. These, it purports, will facilitate continuity from the EYFS into the primary phase and create opportunities for children to apply their knowledge and skills across curriculum areas. In the proposed curriculum, language and literacy comes under the area: understanding English, communication and languages. The other five areas are: mathematical understanding, scientific and technological understanding, historical, geographical and social understanding, understanding physical development, health and well-being, and understanding the arts. The importance of speaking and listening and planning for language development is also emphasized in the report as fundamental to learning.

What might literacy planning for these areas of learning or cross-curricular links look like? Some teachers may already use a curriculum map or planning grid in order to ensure that they are embedding non-fiction genres in literacy across the curriculum in their medium-term planning. For example, a recount may take the form of a biographical account in history such as an extract from the autobiography of Mary Seacole. On a grid, teachers will plot where they will apply each genre in different subject areas (Figure 9.3). They may also do the same for narrative and poetry.

	Discussion	Explanation	Instruction	Persuasion	Recount	Report
Art						
Citizenship						
D & T						
Geography						
History						
MFL						
Music						
Numeracy						
P.E.						
R.E.						
Science						

Figure 9.3   Example of a curriculum planning map

Task box

The text you will be planning from for Year 5 is *The Street Child* by Berlie Doherty. The book is based on a true story of a street orphan who inspired Dr Barnado to eventually set up children's homes. It also enables children to understand issues of child labour and poverty. The unit of work may last three weeks. Can you plan some teaching and learning activities which are inclusive and stimulating, which will embed language and literacy learning across some subject areas?

(Continued)

(Continued)

Considerations

When planning using a cross-curricular approach, it is best to choose a children's text or area that inspires genuine connections across subjects. We have seen how important it is to ensure there are opportunities for drama and talk. You will also have to think about the forms of writing that will be appropriate (such as a diary for a recount or a poster advertising a persuasive text). Also, consider how you will build in progression and bridge learning with relevant, cultural contexts using the same theme.

Planning communication, language and literacy in the EYFS

Planning for language and literacy in the EYFS means teaching and assessing children's experiences in the six areas of learning from 0 to 5 years. One of these areas 'Communication, language and literacy' is divided further into: Language for Communication, Language for Thinking, Linking Sounds and Letters, Reading, Writing and Handwriting. Key to this, is bringing first-hand experiences to life. It is important to plan a balance of activities which are child or adult led, as well as planning for the use of the outdoor environment and visits to places that will stimulate language and literacy development. The positive effects of planning sensory experiences which motivate children's language development are outlined in research by the Forest Schools, downloadable at www.forestresearch.gov.uk. These are increasing in popularity throughout Britain, particularly with early years practitioners.

Debate in planning for 'Linking Sounds to Letters' has centred mainly on two early learning goals (ELGs) that children need to attain by the end of the Foundation Stage, which some teachers have said are inappropriate for early learners. Controversy also surrounds the Rose Report (2006) recommendations, which strongly advised teachers to adopt a synthetic phonics approach to teaching reading. Emphasis when planning reading opportunities for very young children should essentially be on developing phonological awareness through talk, storytelling, rhyme and alliteration.

Medium-term planning means using the 2008 Practice Guidance for the Early Years Foundation Stage principles, which are grouped into four themes: A Unique Child, Positive Relationships, Enabling Environments, and Learning and Development. Planning should be informed by ongoing assessments with teaching colleagues, parents and outside agencies. The document by the DfES (2007a) entitled *Supporting Children Learning English as an Additional Language in the Early Years Foundation Stage*, shows what effective practice might look like for each theme. It also refers to potential challenges and dilemmas when planning for inclusion of bilingual learners. For example, when planning for 'A Unique Child', it is important to understand that bilingual learners are not a homogenous group and that you will need to work closely with parents so that vital information can be shared about any child. This may, in turn, involve the challenge of accessing suitable translation and interpreting facilities so that you can communicate effectively with parents and carers.

Short-term planning or weekly planning will relate to the stepping stones and ELGs from the curriculum guidance. An example of an ELG in Language for Communication is: 'Listen with enjoyment, and respond to stories, songs and other music, rhymes and poems and make up their own stories, songs, rhymes and poems.'

Task box

What language and literacy activities and resources could you use in your weekly planning in order to begin to address this ELG? Notice the emphasis on 'enjoyment' and 'inventiveness'.

The assessment cycle at this early stage involves the teacher engaging in a process called 'Look, listen, note'.

Essentially, teachers will plan to observe children in each area of learning and make notes accordingly. Unlike a tick sheet, this will be a record of a child's learning journey and it will be used to inform planning and resourcing.

When observing language for communication for example, comments would be made about a child's growing vocabulary and grammar, their use of first language, gestures and body language. Notes could also be made on their knowledge of rhymes and songs and awareness of conventions such as turn taking.

Assessment for learning and the planning cycle

All reflective practitioners should be seeking and interpreting evidence to decide *where the learners are in their learning, where they need to go and how best to get there* (Assessment Reform Group, 2002). All teachers, when planning for language and literacy development need to reflect on the teaching, planning and assessment for learning cycle.

The important thing to remember when planning is that ongoing assessment of children's language and literacy learning will inform planning the next steps in their learning. Plans will then be annotated, the context and time taken and evidence of learning jotted down, with an analysis of the language and literacy competence of individual children, including miscues in reading, misconceptions and other evidence.

Using recommended assessment for learning strategies, teachers are encouraged to share learning objectives with children and then generate smaller steps of how to achieve these objectives with children. These smaller steps are known as 'success criteria'. An example of a learning objective in Year 3 might be: *Design an instructional text, using the appropriate structure and language features.* The related success criteria could be: *Use imperatives; make sure the instructions are in the correct order; organize the text clearly.* A word of warning on the overuse of success criteria however: this may stifle children's creativity and limit what they can do.

Planning creatively in language and literacy

Following the 'post-strategy teaching world' and teacher as a 'deliverer of learning' (Lambirth, 2006), teachers have far greater freedom again to plan creatively in language and literacy. Initiatives from the Qualifications and Curriculum Authority such as Creativity: Find it! Promote! (QCA, 2005) encourage planning which fosters children's creativity, focusing on the creative *process* rather than the *product*. Teachers are actively encouraged to be flexible in their planning and adapt the Primary National Strategy learning objectives to suit the learners they teach. Ken Robinson, whose Technology, Entertainment and Design (TED) lecture on creativity has been watched millions of times (downloadable at http://www.ted.com/index.php/talks/ken_robinson_says_schools_kill_creativity.html) looks at conditions that enable us to be 'in the zone' and which unlock children's creative potential.

How can this become part of planning in language and literacy? In fact, as we have seen, by planning inclusive lessons for bilingual learners, many teachers are already planning creatively by:

- devising activities that are culturally and personally authentic
- planning for a range of teaching and learning styles so that children can experience high levels of involvement and engage their creativity
- planning for role play, discussion, experiential learning, problem-solving and collaborative activities
- setting challenging, but achievable goals with meaningful contexts
- creating a fun, secure, yet risk taking culture of learning
- being prepared to alter plans, following children's interests, and change tack
- modelling creative thinking and behaviour

- inviting members of the local community, authors and writers who share the creative process with children and bring literacy to life
- encouraging questions, open discussions, the sharing of ideas
- planning the use of resources such as film, digital texts, the Internet, computer games, artefacts and an environment which inspires creative learning.

Indeed, the question may not only be to just discover who you are, as Ken Robinson (2009) suggests, but to find out who your children are, so that you can plan for all their needs and interests effectively.

Bringing all the elements together: planning an effective literacy lesson

A teacher's daily language and literacy planning will include some of the following key elements:

- Language and literacy objectives using child friendly language. These will consider vocabulary, grammar and functional use of language. Links will be made explicit to objectives in the National Curriculum, EYFS or Primary Framework for Literacy.
- Stimulating starting points which take account of children's texts, film, visitors who inspire learning.
- Links with prior language and literacy learning:

  - including competence in speaking, listening, reading and writing in a child's first language
  - using personal stories from different cultural backgrounds.

- Whole-class teaching with:

  - high cognitive challenge set in meaningful, relevant contexts
  - use of rhyme, rhythm and story telling for younger children
  - speaking and listening interrelated with reading and writing
  - modelling or demonstration of new language and literacy learning
  - engaging literacy resources which encourage children's creativity.

- Guided or independent work which:

  - scaffolds reading and writing tasks effectively
  - differentiates by a variety of means – by task, language support, teaching and learning style
  - builds in opportunities for play, the outdoor environment and sustained, shared conversations in the early years
  - uses culturally appropriate literacy resources which cater for the needs of individuals and groups of learners.

- Plenary sessions, including mini plenaries which:
    - review learning and challenge children to explain or justify their ideas
    - use a range of strategies to assess children's learning against language and learning objectives
    - encourage dialogue and feedback on literacy learning.

What does this mean when planning language learning for bilingual pupils?

As we have already seen, clear learning objectives are crucial to successful planning. When planning for the needs of bilingual children, you will also need to consider language learning objectives and adopt a teaching style which allows children to rehearse and use language in meaningful contexts. You will need to be wary of thinking of bilingual learners as having a deficit, or indeed a 'barrier' to learning and always in need of support, which is implied by some of the terminology. The key to planning for all children is to keep the challenge high, while contextualizing the task with:

- visual prompts such as pictures or artefacts
- information and communication technology resources including inter-active whiteboard resources, digital video, games and e-books
- speaking and listening strategies, including role play and drama
- writing frames (Wray and Lewis, 1997)
- concept maps which represent ideas by displaying categories of information
- KWL grids (What do I KNOW about this topic? What do I WANT to know? What did I LEARN?) (Wray and Lewis, 1997) which divide information into what children **k**now, what they **w**ant to know and what they have **l**earnt.

The most recent documentation by the Primary National Strategy has outlined three core principles that should inform all language and literacy learning:

- Bilingualism is an asset and the first language continues to play a significant role in acquiring an additional language.
- Cognitive challenge should be kept high, through linguistics and contextual support which 'scaffold' learning.
- Language acquisition goes hand in hand with cognitive and academic development with an inclusive curriculum as the context (DfES, 2006b).

The role of Interdependence theory

Theories of additional language acquisition should underpin effective language and literacy planning. The following provides insight into one of the most influential ways of thinking about learners of English as an additional language.

Theory snapshot

The theoretical framework that is most widely used to inform planning for bilingual learners is Jim Cummins's interdependence theory of bilingualism. Cummins is a Canadian educationalist and researcher who examined the interplay between language development and the cognitive and academic domain.

He distinguishes between 'basic interpersonal communication skills' (BICS) and 'cognitive and academic language proficiency' (CALP). Cummins's work highlights the important role of the first language in the child's learning and in their acquisition of additional languages.

All children develop conversational skills first, in face-to-face highly contextualized situations, but take longer to develop the language which contributes to educational success. Cummins acknowledged that some interpersonal communication can impose considerable cognitive demands on a speaker and that academic situations may also require social communication skills. Generally speaking, children learning an additional language can become conversationally fluent in the new language in two to three years but it may take five years or longer to catch up with monolingual peers on the development of CALP.

Those who have developed CALP in their first language can transfer much of this learning to additional languages. Children who move into a new language environment at an early age can benefit enormously if they are given opportunities to continue to develop their first language alongside English, using both languages for cognitively demanding tasks.

The distinction between these two types of language and their rates of development is now recognized in the Office for Standards in Education (Ofsted) framework for inspecting English as an additional language (EAL) in Primary Schools (Ofsted, 2008). Development of the theory into two dimensions (Figure 9.4) has further implications for planning for bilingual learners. The quadrants effectively enable teachers to consider whether the tasks they are planning are context embedded or context reduced and/or cognitively undemanding or demanding.

In short, bilingual learners face two main tasks in school: they need to learn English and they need to learn the content of the curriculum. These tasks must proceed hand in hand.

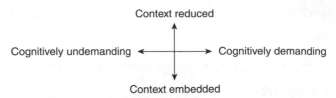

Figure 9.4 A theoretical framework for relating language proficiency to academic achievement
Source: Adapted from: Cummins (1984)

Criticism of BICS and CALP has focused on the possibility that the terminology suggests compartmentalization and oversimplification. Basic interpersonal communication skills may be regarded by some as inferior to CALP (Wiley, 2005) and a bilingual learner's language competencies are far more dynamic and complex, depending on the environment, language domain and use of bilingual ability. Socio-economic class and sociocultural differences were not part of Cummins's original theory.

Planning frameworks

One of the clearest and most systematic frameworks for planning for bilingual learners, which was underpinned by this theoretical understanding of language acquisition, was that produced by Gravelle (2000) (Figure 9.5).

	What do learners bring to the task?	What does the task demand of them?	What support needs to be planned?
Social			
Cognitive			
Linguistic			

Figure 9.5 A framework for planning
Source: Gravelle (2000)

This framework is useful in that it draws attention to issues that are of particular relevance to bilingual learners. For example, children have prior social experiences, cognitive understanding and first language learning that they will bring with them to a planned task. It is important to find out a learner's proficiency in all four language skills – speaking, listening, reading and writing – and how fluent they are in each of these, in the languages they are competent in. As you have seen in Chapter 1, all language learning involves social interaction and cognitive and language development. When planning, it is therefore important to think about how you will group children. It may be beneficial to place an early bilingual child in a group with another child who speaks their first language, although social and emotional needs will also have to be considered when grouping children.

Teachers will also consider the cognitive demands of the task. The National Literacy Strategy analyses the language demands of a task by looking at word, sentence and text level objectives. However, when planning language learning with bilingual pupils, it is also useful to consider three basic elements: vocabulary, grammar and functions of language.

1 *Vocabulary.* What is the key vocabulary of the text that you want them to know in order for them to be able to understand it? Once they have acquired the key vocabulary, learners can then apply the same vocabulary in a speaking and listening, reading or writing task and a different curriculum context.

2 *Grammar*. What are the grammatical structures? Is the text composed using particular grammatical structures? For example, a recount in the form of a diary will be written mainly in the past tense. Are there grammatical structures that a learner of a specific language may find particularly difficult? What are the more challenging language structures? For example, the connectives 'and' and 'but' are basic connectives, whereas connectives like 'although' and 'however' are more complex. The passive tense is a more difficult language structure to acquire and for learners to process. This is evident in the sentence: A number of factors were indicated by these results.

3 *Functions*. What are the language functions of the task? Functions of language are linked to genre theory, which was first expounded by linguists who were working in the field of discourse analysis. For example, when sorting information, a learner will be 'classifying' or when using the language of advertising, 'persuading'. The key to this perspective is that children use language in order to be able to function (Halliday, 1975).

In literacy planning, the genres are often referred to as 'text types', with particular language features. There are also a variety of 'forms', such as posters or advertisements for persuasive genre. The text types as outlined by the Primary Strategy (DFES, 2006a) are narrative, instructional/procedural, explanatory, persuasion, discussion, non-chronological reports and recount. Text types are used in combination with one another and there is now a general consensus of opinion that there can be a mix of genres in literacy. However, awareness of genre theory is important when planning, teaching and assessing early bilingual learners who are in the initial stage of learning how a new language works. Familiarizing children with the language and culture afforded by these texts is crucial for all learners, but particularly bilingual learners. As children internalize the conventions and become familiar with these text types, they will become more adept at talking and designing their own writing.

Summary

- Integrating the core literacy strands of speaking, listening, reading and writing is at the heart of effective planning in literacy.
- Children's texts on paper or on screen should be the starting point for literacy learning. Knowing the texts that will engage children, yet provide the necessary learning context for language skills, knowledge and understanding is the key to making literacy stimulating.
- For all learners, language and literacy is consolidated through its application across the curriculum. Teachers usually map these literacy links in cross-curricular approaches when planning.
- Planning for creatively needs teachers to first model creative thinking and behaviour and endeavour to build a culture which fosters creativity in action.
- Planning literacy learning in the Foundation Stage means planning for the area of learning called, 'Communication, language and literacy'. Activities will be adult or children led and provide a variety of multi-sensory and first-hand experiences.
- Medium-term planning in literacy takes place over several weeks in a 'unit of work'. This could be narrative, non-narrative or poetry.

Short term planning in literacy occurs over a week or a series of individual lessons. Assessment for learning is fundamental to the planning process using language and literacy objectives that are clear and comprehensible to children. Weekly plans will be annotated and adapted according to children's needs and interests.

Understanding learning theory is the basis of planning, teaching and assessing. Applying Cummins's theory of interdependence will enable you to think about the cognitive, academic and language demands of literacy tasks that you plan and contextualize and support them appropriately.

Concluding comments

Ansell is able to provide us with a strong overview of planning for language and literacy with inclusion in a central position. This is a valuable set of outlines for thinking about planning and as it is placed at the end of the book I am sure that you now have enough insight to tackle the career-long development of a planning system that serves you, your pupils and the other professionals that you work with perfectly!

CHAPTER 10

PRIMARY ENGLISH CURRICULUM PERSPECTIVES

CHRIS ROBERTSON

This final chapter is a little different in nature from the first nine – it seeks to provide a semi-colon to the rest of the book; a moment where the reader can pause and reflect on life-long aspects of learning to teach. It also gives an insight into where your career might lead you.

This chapter is written by the Head of an Institute of Education in a British University who has been tasked with managing provision of Initial Teacher Education and those striving for qualified teacher status (QTS). It is intended to give an insight into how one career in teaching has evolved and how, at no matter what level we are involved in the education of children, we are all linked by a collective purpose – which is to provide the best possible classroom experiences for young children.

This final chapter presents a life journey – the story of me, as a gifted primary English teacher and my journey through the curriculum labyrinth of the last 40 years to the end of the first decade of the new millennium. In particular this chapter seeks to present my story and capture the mediation between my personal voice and the wider cultural and curriculum imperatives of the teaching of English language in the primary school.

When I began teaching there was a curriculum culture which already existed: the teaching of English albeit in the guise of reading and writing has been a part of the curriculum taught in schools since time immemorial. The early printed lesson books for children in the nineteenth and early twentieth centuries reflected a strong emphasis on both these elements of English but are interesting for the greater contribution reading and writing made to moral education rather than their contribution to learning. Speaking and listening as we know it in schools today would have been discouraged in a the culture which existed at the time of 'children should be seen and not heard' with mantras such as 'speak when you are spoken to'. The 3Rs of 'reading, writing and arithmetic' dominated the curriculum from the early twentieth century through to the 1950s when in primary schools the curriculum broadened to include a wider range of subjects including history, geography, art and music.

By the 1970s the English primary curriculum had begun to veer away from the formal English teaching which preceded it. I had had experience of some very formal English teaching of grammar and sentence analysis (parsing) as a grammar school pupil and lessons in Latin, in retrospect provided me with a very good grounding in the structure of language that enabled me to learn other languages without too much difficulty. It also provided me with the knowledge and understanding required to teach English well, though the pedagogy adopted certainly was not engaging, let alone inspirational. In contrast, I had been particularly fortunate as a primary-aged pupil attending a small rural primary school in North Wales, to have experienced as a 10-year-old the delights of such a gifted storyteller as my class teacher. Ilid Williams filled every day with wonderful stories and readings: his reading of Tom Sawyer grasped my imagination and I sat immersed in Tom's amazing story set in the southern states of America during the slave trade, a million miles away from my own experience of life in distance and in time. I can still see Mr Williams's left eyebrow which he raised periodically to punctuate a particular thought-provoking passage or phrase as he sat perched on a desk, his feet resting on a chair, storybook casually held in one hand, the magic of a shared world in the air. He created an ambience for us, where, 'the writer's sense of audience and the reader's sense of textual voice complement each other and form a social bond' (Benton and Fox, 1985: 2). I just had to buy that book for myself with my pocket money, as though to possess some of that magic, not just of the story but also to hear the voice of Mr Williams reading it in my head as I read it for myself!

Like Mr Williams, I have always sought to capture my pupils in the story I have been reading and to help them find authors and books which enable them to engage fully with the narrative when reading independently. This, I believe, 'hooks' children on reading and books so that it becomes a lifelong pleasure, not a chore. If the story-maker is truly skilled in his or her art, then the reader 'enters a "secondary world" and "inside it" if, what he (the storyteller) relates is "true": it accords with the laws of that world. You therefore believe it, while you are, as it were, inside. The moment disbelief arises, the spell is broken, the magic, or rather the art, has failed' (Tolkien, 1964: 36).

Here are some voices of teachers and trainee teachers reflecting on their experience of learning to read: a chore or a pleasure?

Reading scheme books were part of the problem ... it wasn't easy. They never appealed to me. 'Real' books were far more enjoyable and plausible. Now, as an adult, books for me are not an escape but an extension of my existence. (Corrine)

I can remember my elder brother bringing his early reading book home from school when he was about 5 and I was still only about 4. One book I particularly recall was 'Old Lott's farm' which I apparently used to adore and learnt from cover to cover. I think it was this keen early interest in books which caused me to become an early reader. I remember trying to write a book myself in the Infants, and I'm still trying. (Mike)

I was an impatient child who quickly became bored. I found reading tiresome. I took 'A level' English when I still read 'Tiger' and 'Roy of the Rovers'! Coriolanus proved a mystery, Romeo was a drip and the altruism in Jane Austen's characters stumped me. ... When on teaching practice.

I empathise with the bored looks on the energetic youngsters faces. Libraries are bland on the whole. (Simon)

I've always been able to read! I cannot remember anything about learning to read only that there was always plenty of reading material at home ... a huge bookcase full of books ... my mother had a regular order of women's magazines which she read ... my elder brother was an avid reader and would read into the early hours ... and would be (still) reading at breakfast (Aileen)

My first memory of reading was having to take a box of flash cards home though my parents say I already read the (news)paper at home probably to see what was on TV ...' (YR2 ITE student) (Robertson, 1994, unpublished journal data)

Such experiences as a pupil made me who I am as a teacher and provided me with both good and bad role models that helped inform my development from pupil to teacher. My A-level English teacher, Mr Brookes, was passionate about his subject to the exclusion of all else, articulate, well read, but very 'mad' and very fearsome if crossed! However, his passion for the novels of Thomas Hardy, Wilfred Owen's war poetry and that of the metaphysical writers, such as John Donne, again inspired me and feeds my creative being and my love of poetry and novels to this day. It confirmed for me that English was my subject!

It was during the 1970s as a young teacher myself that I embarked enthusiastically on an English curriculum, determined mostly by me, which included creative writing, interpretive writing, story reading, shared reading time, discussion and dialogic talk, poetry and drama, inspired by educationalists, linguists and philosophers of the period. Teaching English to primary-aged children confirmed a joy and passion in language and watching language develop in children, which has remained with me throughout my career in teaching and education. I ought to confess that my curriculum also had, not surprisingly, a strong emphasis on books and learning to read. Reading stories, listening to stories, encouraging children to share the many delights of children's literature and poetry, as well as listening to children read and talking about their books, was highly evident in my approach to teaching. This focus was strongly influenced by my own love of books and further predicated on a personal philosophy influenced by psycholinguistics and informed by the writings of theorists such as Frank Smith (1984), Bettelheim (1975, 1981), Bruner (1986, 1990), Applebee (1978, 1987), Meek (1982, 1988; Meek et al., 1977), Wells (1986), Chomsky (1957), Donaldson (1989) and many other influential writers and thinkers of that era, too numerous to mention (see Chapter 3 on reading). This philosophy and my passion for encouraging children as learners to become 'hooked on reading' flooded through my teaching. My own meticulous systems of observation, assessment and record-keeping (devised long before the National Curriculum imposed its own standard assessment tasks in 1988), and dialogic interaction with my pupils and their parents/carers, provided me with evidence that as a teacher of English I was providing very successfully for the learning needs of my children and they were reading, writing and discussing with confidence, understanding, skill and flair, dependent on their developing ability.

And the voices of children whom I have taught, talking about reading and about books ...

In response to, 'What goes on in your head when you are reading?':

I see people in my head (5-year-old)

Yes, especially when they haven't go pictures, I make my own pictures up in my head ... coloured sometimes, not normally coloured. I see six red wizards but they're not red in the book (6-year-old)

In the Valley of Adventure, I could see the cave and the waterfall (9-year-old)

When I go out into the playground, I am batman (8-year-old)

Like a TV programme in my head ... the quality of the book makes good pictures (11-year-old)

Robertson, 1995: 44

As moving around the country took me to different schools and local authorities, I became suddenly very aware of new and unfamiliar approaches to teaching reading including 'i.t.a.' (the initial teaching alphabet) and various evolutions of this method of teaching reading. One teacher wrote in my journal about her experience of 'i.t.a' as a pupil, 'I learnt to read via the i.t.a. I remember thinking it did not look like normal writing'. Although she mastered reading books using ita, she still felt she could 'not read properly ... the transition from i.t.a. to

normal reading was not very easy but with perseverance I managed'
(Judy) (for more information about this Initial Teaching Alphabet common at this time see http://www.smecc.org/ita.htm). Such schemes were
not teacher-led and though questioned at the time, they were enforced
quite strongly in some local authorities and schools, leaving teachers
somewhat powerless.

Similarly, while teaching in Sunderland I was introduced for the first
time to what I considered to be a truly alien method of teaching reading (and writing/spelling) where each sound was allocated its own colour.
Consequently, for writing on the blackboard I had to have a large supply of coloured chalks (no interactive whiteboard then) which had to be
interchanged rapidly as I led the lesson, managed a class of 35 boisterous
children, remembered the sequence of my lesson and juggled the chalks.
As though this was not challenging enough, teaching children with very
strong Geordie accents meant my accent (or rather non-Geordie accent)
pronounced sounds, including dipthongs, very differently to them,
and when teaching phonics this certainly confused matters – another
steep learning curve for me in my second year of teaching and I quickly
changed how I spoke! Although I loved my time spent in the north-east,
I certainly had no regrets leaving this method of teaching reading and
writing behind.

When we moved to the Midlands I breathed a sigh of relief and began
to come to terms with other, as it seemed to me, regional fads and fet-
ishes which existed in the English curriculum. My first head teacher in a
Birmingham school was adamant that in his school, children, and therefore staff, could do beautiful cursive writing and copy write perfectly, with
handwriting lessons being timetabled daily and observed by him frequently.
Thus I quickly adapted from the multicoloured disjointed print to a flow-
ing cursive style under his watchful eye. Apart from such local and sometimes regional school policy foci, the curriculum design which I delivered
remained my own responsibility and allowed me to be creative and innovative. So long as my class scored highly on the Schonell standardized reading tests, wrote their cursive scripts neatly and completed endless boring
comprehension tests, known as 'SRA', as prescribed within the school policy, then all was well. My classes loved listening to Dahl's *James and the
Giant Peach*, C. Day Lewis's, *Lion, the Witch and the Wardrobe*, Burnett's
Secret Garden and other stories by Nina Bawden, Phillipa Pearce, Leon
Garfield and Dick King-Smith. They loved listening to and writing poetry,
in fact writing in all its forms (exploratory, persuasive, argument etc) and
taking part in drama and performance. At this time, the whole curriculum
was very much cross-curricular and project based, which enabled me to
develop my writing, reading and speaking curriculum in a holistic and purposeful way – happy times despite the enforced cursive or should that be
'cursed' writing!

And the voices of children whom I have taught, talking about what makes a good story ...

because it has a happy ending ... starts with a good start .. characters ... I like animals ... lions. (6-year-old)

Active.. nasty in the middle ... it starts to get nasty and then it gets happy, for example, a storm rocking a boat, or you fall in the canal. (7-year-old)

It has to be lively and interesting with more than two people in it ... the way they write it ... full stops, commas ...not boring like: the ... pig ... went ...to ...the ..super ...mar ...ket!' (9-year-old).

Characters are clever, interesting ... the story tells you what they are trying to do ... the plot should be to the point and have imagination. (11-year-old)

A move to Shropshire brought me in contact with the Talk project (1980s) and then the National Oracy project (Wilkinson, 1980) which I thought was wonderful and enlightening, empowering pupils to engage more fully in their learning. The influence of Don Holdaway (1979, 1980) on this project was significant although his writing had been originally published in the 1960s. As a teacher I maintained my psycholinguistic approach to teaching reading and as a successful teacher of reading enjoyed promotion and diversification to take on other roles, including working with children with language difficulties and building up my expertise in this area at County level for many years. The sociocultural philosophy of teaching and learning, research and writing by Vygotsky (1962, 1978), Wells (1986), Darling-Hammond and Bransford (2005), Mercer and Littleton (2007), and Mercer (in Alexander, 2010) also impacted significantly on my understanding of learning in and out of the classroom. Major influences on the primary English curriculum at this time included 'paired reading', 'shared reading', and whole-class 'uninterrupted sustained, silent reading (USSR) time'. This last model usually took place in school for the first half hour after lunch when everyone, including the teacher, supposedly engaged in silent or quiet reading. My own later research (Robertson et al., 1996) into the rhetoric and practice of sustained silent reading in primary schools across three English counties revealed that the practice undertaken by some teachers and in some classrooms was very far from the model which was being prescribed or described/understood by the teachers themselves. At around the same time the 'reading recovery programme' (Clay, 1979, 1985) entered the curriculum. Originating initially in New Zealand, it quickly spread throughout the UK as the panacea to address reading delay or difficulties. While based on sound principles and research, including long-term observations of children by Clay, it became distilled into an overly mechanistic prescription to cure all reading ills, 'a quick fix'.

Then the English National Curriculum appeared on the horizon in 1989. 'The nature of the primary school curriculum and the climate in which schools function changed quite dramatically following the passing of the Education Reform Act in 1988' (Ashcroft and Palacio, 1997: 2) and yellow was the coloured assigned to English, an appropriate sunny colour, I thought. Again English was subdivided into reading, writing and speaking and listening. Although for me these were all familiar and important aspects to develop in the classroom, many teachers, new and highly experienced, struggled with the latter as unchartered and unfriendly water. So we struggled with the reconceptualization of reading while others had little understanding of English and its forms. Grammar and syntax were alien to some and something older teachers had never had to engage with, perhaps even since they were pupils in school themselves, while younger teachers brought up on a more liberal creative writing curriculum, often devoid of any formal grammar teaching, had escaped any formal contact with such things in their own education. Though using the English language correctly in spoken and written form, some had had little experience of its explicit features, structures and nuances.

As a primary teacher and then working in the County Advisory Service supporting children, families and schools with language and literacy problems, I was able to negotiate the requirement of the English National Curriculum to support professional development and learning for teachers and others working in the classroom, such as teaching assistants. The inclusion of reading, writing and speaking and listening, was helpful in supporting my own philosophy of language learning and development. Broadening what has often been, a narrow range of genres that teachers and their pupils had engaged with brought opportunities for exciting exploration by teachers in their classrooms as to what children might do. Raising the profile of children with learning difficulties and children for whom English was an additional language was welcomed. Although philosophically it was still a long way from the 'Every Child Matters' agenda (DfES, 2004b), it helped raise the profile, backed by legal requirements, of meeting the needs of all children. The National Curriculum despite its many critics helped to raise the profile of English and the teaching skills of teachers through a national programme of staff development. Delivering professional development for teachers in areas of language, literacy and SEN (inclusion) was an enjoyable and rewarding part of my work, particularly when able to observe at first hand the improvements in learning and teaching.

However, one cannot discuss the National Curriculum without consideration of the very strict testing and benchmarking regime which accompanied it, and some of the early criticisms focused more on this than on the curriculum itself. Philosophically many teachers rebelled at the thought of a prescribed curriculum which took away individual freedom to respond to both the real context and situations of different classrooms and their pupils. The national testing and standard assessment tasks (SATs) that were imposed were, and still are, often considered to be mechanical, stressful and lacking validity or reliability in their outcome. However, publishing SATs results and school leagues tables gave schools a stronger reason for focusing on 'performing well'. Unfortunately, in working with children with learning and/or behaviour difficulties, it was quickly apparent that as these national league tables were published so, in some schools, low-achieving children gradually became more and more regarded as a negative input on the school's performance. Exclusion of children therefore began to rise and those schools with a greater commitment to policies of inclusion became, over time, a 'dumping' ground for the more difficult children to teach and manage. One could say that this focus on constantly measuring results and 'weighing the pig to see if it's put on weight' has detracted from the real focus of allowing teachers to teach and children to learn.

During this period I moved from teaching and leading others in schools to operate effectively and creatively within the National Curriculum requirements to teaching the requirement of the English curriculum to initial teacher training (ITT) students in a university. Those readers of this chapter, familiar with ITT, may be surprised to learn that in the 1990s the government for a period of a few years imposed a very rigid English curriculum on providers of ITT. This was in addition to the required outcomes of training, that is Standards for Qualified Teacher Status (QTS), which remain today. Thus, schools were not the only institutions to wrestle with an imposed, central curriculum. As part of my university teaching I taught Masters programmes for teachers in 'Reading', 'Writing' and 'Speaking and Listening'. Working with teachers and trainee teachers who were themselves 'learners' emphasized for me the importance of helping both groups to develop as inspirational teachers of English. In this way I believed I could make a greater difference in the classroom itself and on the lives of all the pupils this group would influence over time, thus, moving up a generation or two, my mission became to inspire teachers and trainees teachers to become 'hooked on books', and 'hooked on teaching and learning language and literacy'.

During this time, I supported many primary teachers and English subject co-ordinators in developing and evaluating their school curriculum policies in English. Sometimes it was evident that policies were themselves constrained by what teachers/schools themselves understood and knew of the potential of the English curriculum. The primary English policy agreed in some schools often bore little resemblance to classroom practice (Keating et al., 1996). Sometimes teachers' own understanding, and sometimes their limited confidence in the subject, put up barriers which prevented them developing their teaching beyond the basic national framework of requirements.

In my experiences throughout this period, although most educationalists and many teachers welcomed the higher profile of speaking and listening in the English curriculum, all the evidence suggests that even today, some 20 years after the introduction of the National Curriculum, teachers still choose to hold the balance in terms of classroom talk, despite the greater awareness of the importance of talk in the learning process (Jones, 1988; Mercer in Alexander, 2010; Tann, 1991; Myhill and Fisher, 2006; Wells, 1986). Much classroom talk remains tokenistic and instructional rather than implicitly dialogic. Speaking and listening, is still sadly neglected in many classrooms and yet research demonstrates repeatedly that 'spoken language forms a constant ceiling not only on the ability to comprehend but also on the ability to write, beyond which literacy cannot progress' (Myhill and Fisher, 2006: 6).

It is through talk and playing with words that we learn to formulate what we really want to say with clarity, whether it be to express an emotion, debate a point, argue the case or describe a scene. The ability to truly articulate intended meaning, as the great T.S. Eliot (1943) proclaims, comes only by making mistakes, stumbling, listening, beginning, stopping, restarting and trying again so that we gradually become more comfortable and confident in the talk process. This is the process in which expert teachers (and expert parents) constantly support their children, providing endless authentic opportunities for speaking and listening.

Again, the voice of T.S. Eliot, a master 'wordsmith', can contribute effectively to this argument:

Trying to learn to use words, and every attempt
Is a wholly new start, and a different kind of failure
Because one has only learnt to get the better of words
For the thing one no longer has to say, or the way in which
One is no longer disposed to say it. And so each venture
Is a new beginning?

(Eliot, 1943, 'East Coker')

The National Curriculum (DfES, 1989) professed to be a 'curriculum for all' and a 'broad and balanced' curriculum, and certainly it raised issues of equality for children with special needs as well as emphasizing the particular needs of children for whom English is an additional language. However, it can be argued that many major educational changes, including those to the curriculum, are driven not by the needs of children and their families but by politicians seeking to gain votes: 'change for change's sake'. In the UK, political parties have indeed had significant impact on the curriculum. For example, the educational reform legislation of 1988, of which the National Curriculum was part, introduced by the then Conservative government, was built on the notion of individual rights where consumer choice and competition would allow greater social mobility. The previous Labour government of the 1960s produced Circular 10/65 (DES, 1965) which suggested that providing a school system built on 'equality of opportunity' would progress education and ensure progression, achievement and a socially just educational system which would ameliorate class distinction.

More recently, New Labour (1997) sought to walk a line between these two versions and focus on developing 'good schools' where achievement, social mobility and the elimination of the achievement gap between rich and poor; and black and white would be evident. The political focus on schools and the curriculum have been significant since the 1980s and schools and the curriculum have undergone significant changes as a result. Shortly after the 1997 election, the new government set ambitious targets for 2002 that 80% of children should achieve at least level 4 in national tests in literacy. Although this was achieved ultimately, it was not until 2008. Policies and the introduction of new initiatives were 'imposed on teachers at a rate which has made their assimilation and implementation nearly impossible. By one count, between 1996 and 2004 government and national agencies issued 459 documents just on literacy teaching' (Hofkins and Northern, 2009: 3).

The concurrent development of strategies and initiatives have indeed multiplied – the numeracy strategy, the literacy strategy and the primary strategy to name but a few that have significant impact on both teachers and pupils in the way subjects have been taught and on the structure and delivery of the actual content of the curriculum. The three part lesson has become the norm – introduction, development and plenary – dominating the majority of classrooms across England. The pace and focus of lessons certainly moved up a gear in many instances but the price for a very focused, controlled lesson structure has often been a neglect of quality time spent on sustained writing or in-depth reading of longer and more complex books. Short, snappy passages may be used to develop particular comprehension skills but without the skill of sustained reading many children will never have developed the skills required to concentrate on reading a book, or to listen to one being read.

Although results at Key Stage 1, 2 and 3 are the best that they have ever been across the broad range of groups, and schools generally appear to be achieving well yet still the focus on change in the curriculum remains. The schools are good; the standards have been raised; yet the machinery for inspection, improvement and reform continues onwards. Literacy and numeracy, however, remain most closely under the political microscope and, since the turn of the twenty-first century, the pace of change in education, schools and the curriculum has not eased up. In the closing stages of Blair's leadership of New Labour a new and clearly focused policy emerged – the *Five Year Strategy for Children and Learners: Maintaining the Excellent*

Progress (DfES, 2004a). Subsequently the mission of the Department for Education and Skills has become:

- A just society, where outcomes are determined by aptitude and ambition, not by circumstances of birth;
- A safe, cohesive society, with young people entering adulthood able to make a positive contribution; and
- A prosperous society, successful in a globalised economy and able to support excellent public services. (DfES, 2004a: 3).

Clearly New Labour was aware of the success of their educational reforms at the micro-level through SATs results and Ofsted inspection results and other measurable achievements, but as New Labour's time in government became limited due to changing leadership and economic pressure, New Labour embarked on an agenda of social reform and with a focus on global impact. The launch of *Every Child Matters* (DfES, 2004b) and the Children Act 2004 shows a strong emphasis on the need for teachers to be more 'aware of the current legal requirements, national policies and guidance on the safeguarding and promotion of well-being of children and young people' (TDA, 2007: 9). The impact of this legislation has been specifically to broaden the remit of teachers and others working with children, and while its impact on the curriculum design has been deep and implicit, it may be less easy to spot explicitly, unlike the three-part lesson, phonics teaching, or 'look, cover, write'. *Excellence and Enjoyment* (DfES, 2003a), the new primary strategy, claimed to encourage creativity, enjoyment in learning and high standards. It also consolidated the literacy and numeracy strategies.

There is, however, something extraordinary which sets this agenda for change apart from other more centrally driven political devices – the tragic outcome for Victoria Climbié and the many other children like her who unfortunately find themselves in similar life-threatening situations – challenged the status quo and generating the substance for change. It has provided an opportunity for the profession to challenge many theories and practices related to the child, the family and education and to transform education and teaching into a profession which truly helps all children achieve their potential, in line with the five interdependent outcomes of *Every Child Matters* (DfES, 2004b: 9): 'be healthy', 'stay safe', 'enjoy and achieve', 'make a positive contribution' and 'achieve economic well-being'.

In my role as Professor and Head of Education at the University of Worcester, working closely with the Training and Development Agency for Schools (TDA) and a group of deans from other universities, on the impact the *Every Child Matters* requirements might have on teacher training programmes, I was able to see in this government policy for change, a positive opportunity to, once again, take a given policy and interpret it to ensure some greater good emerges, first for children and young people but also for families, schools and the wider workforce. Putting the child back in to the centre of our educational and social endeavours, supported by powerful national policy-drivers, provided us with an opportunity that we could not afford to miss. The interdisciplinary requirements of the *Every Child Matters* (DfES, 2004b) agenda inevitably impact fundamentally on traditional ways of working which have existed since the 1980s, with each discipline maintaining strong professional/academic boundaries separating it from the next and each protecting its identity. It challenges this 'silo' mentality at its core.

At the macro level, is the imperative of impacting positively on issues of social and educational disadvantage, including inclusion, while, at the micro level, teachers at the chalkface have a probably 'once in a lifetime' opportunity to grasp the empowerment being offered: to ensure that sound educational and social principles do underpin the curriculum we offer and that the child and the development of that individual child is at the heart of what we do as teachers and educators. The voice of the child has never been louder, more compelling or more powerful, therefore this is an opportunity to really ensure speaking and listening is truly at the heart of learning in the much more interactive and dialogic pedagogy which I hope will emerge.

However, the unceasing attack on reading standards by the right over this whole period from 1975 to 2006 and beyond not surprisingly produced another review of early reading, a government commissioned review undertaken by Jim Rose, which grappled with the debate regarding the place of phonics in the teaching of reading. Such debates and supposedly new approaches seem to me, as a practising teacher during this whole period, rather futile and cyclical in nature, producing policies which appear sometimes far distant from the reality of the child struggling to read and write. As politicians strive to find something politically new which will make a difference, so we are sometimes faced with the situation of 'the more things change, the more they stay the same'. On the other hand, we sometimes 'lose the baby as well as the bath water'. Taking a fresh look at how things are done and evaluating them effectively has to be at the heart of effective teaching, and an essential part of being a reflective practitioner.

In addition, we are learning more and at an ever increasing pace about the way we learn and the ways children learn. Neuro-science is teaching us more about how the brain works and how this affects our understanding and knowledge of learning and child development, including language development. The Cambridge Primary Review Research Surveys, (Alexander, 2009a, 2009b) provide us with some thought-provoking and challenging evidence for us as teachers and educators to reflect on. As continuing learners, effective and reflective teachers will want to rethink their approaches to what we do, including how we teach English. Not least, are new technologies contributing to changes in how we communicate as a society, all part of the exciting dynamism of language and literacy teaching. So, nothing stays still, nor would we want it to! However, rushing forward with sometimes ill-considered approaches (as outlined even in my journey through my years as a teacher) can only disadvantage the children who can least afford it, the very many socially and educationally disadvantaged children and young people in our schools.

With the emphasis now centring firmly on the child and his or her needs, the government once again believed an overhaul of the curriculum itself was timely and commissioned the Rose Review of the primary curriculum (Rose, 2009). The changing context similarly empowered academics and professionals themselves to undertake a major review of the curriculum and the Cambridge review (Alexander, 2009a) emerged. The findings of the two reviews philosophically conflict in how the future of primary education and its curriculum should be determined, though perhaps the media have decided to make more of the differences as agreement and similarities would of course not be newsworthy. Alexander's report proposes 12 aims grounded in its evidence and advocates that these 'aims should drive curriculum, pedagogy and school life rather than be tagged on as an afterthought. The review wants its proposed aims to be properly debated, and presents them as a carefully considered alternative to the "off the shelf" approach taken by the Rose review' (Alexander, 2009b: 1). 'Too often, as the review has shown, policy has been introduced without proper evaluation of previous initiatives or on the basis of faulty diagnosis of the problem being tackled' (Hofkins and Northen, 2009: 8). The review advocates a curriculum which 'guarantees children's entitlement to breadth, depth and balance, and to high standards in all the proposed domains, not just some of them and which ensures that language, literacy and oracy are paramount'. Innovatively it proposes combining a national framework with a locally devised community curriculum' (ibid.). Possibly most controversially in terms of the current prescribed curriculum is the proposed winding up of the primary national strategies, reintegrating literacy and literacy with the rest of the curriculum (ibid.).

The latter again reminds me of the more holistic approach teachers had before the National Curriculum was devised, where the integrated curriculum benefited from using language (that is teaching English) across subjects as well as sometimes discretely. However, I would not deny that some brilliant innovations, new understandings and developments in the curriculum, along with technology, do put us in a much more informed and 'better' place than we were in the 1970s and early 1980s. So as teachers of the future, whatever stage we are at in our careers (trainee, newly qualified, experienced, expert or on the verge of retirement) to me the important message is to keep an open and critical mind, reflect and critically evaluate whatever we are being asked to do as teachers, engage with professional learning and research at every opportunity, and be prepared to challenge both our own and others' preconceptions and misconceptions that are not evidence based. The education of children and the central place of language and literacy are too important for us to even consider pulling down the shutters!

To quote David Hawkins, American philosopher and educationalist (in Armstrong, 2010: 3), who wrote of how the best English primary schools were committed to what he described as:

> a major reorganisation of subject matter into a common and coherent framework. The sand and water and clay, the painting and writing and reading, the cooking and building and calculation, the observing and nurture of plants and animals, are woven together into a complex social pattern which sustains romance as it extends a concern for detail and for generalisation.

Teachers of the young are not always given the credit they deserve for the intricate weaving they undertake with children as part of the learning process and 'yet the skilful among them are able to see order and number, geography and history, moral testing grounds and aesthetic qualities in all the encounters of young children with the furniture of a rich environment' (Hawkins, 1973, in Armstrong, 2010: 3).

REFERENCES

Alexander, R.J. (2001) *Culture and Pedagogy: International Comparisons in Primary Education*. Oxford: Blackwell.

Alexander, R.J. (2008) *Towards Dialogic Teaching. Rethinking Classroom Talk* (4th edn). York: Dialogos.

Alexander, R. (ed.) (2009a) *Children, their World, their Education: Final Report and Recommendations of the Cambridge Primary Review*. London: Routledge.

Alexander, R. (ed.) (2009b) *Cambridge Review Briefings: The Final Report*. www.primaryreview.org.uk

Alexander, R. (ed.) (2010) *The Cambridge Review Research Surveys*. London: Routledge.

Alexander, R., Rose, J. and Woodhead, C. (1992) *Curriculum Organisation and Classroom Practice in Primary Schools*. London: DES.

Applebee, A.N. (1978) *Becoming a Reader*. Chicago: University of Chicago Press.

Applebee, A.N. (1987) *The Child's Concept of Story*. Chicago, IL: University of Chicago Press.

Armstrong, M. (2010) 'A personal response to the Cambridge primary review', paper written for the Bristol Cambridge Review Conference, January.

Ashcroft, K. and Palacio, D. (eds) (1997) *Implementing the Primary Curriculum: a Teacher's Guide*. London: Falmer Press.

Assessment Reform Group (ARG) (2006) *Testing, Motivation and Learning*. Cambridge: University of Cambridge School of Education, Assessment Reform Group.

Baker, M. (2005) 'Who could be right about reading?', *BBC News*, 9 April.

Barnett, A., Henderson, S., Scheib, B. and Schulz (2007) *Detailed Assessment of Speed of Handwriting* (DASH). Oxford: Harcourt Assessment.

Barnett, A., Stainthorp, R., Henderson, S. and Scheib, B. (2006) *Handwriting Policy and Practice in English Primary Schools*. London: Institute of Education Publications.

Barrs, M. and Cork, V. (2001) *The Reader in the Writer*. London: CLPE.

Bearne, E. (2002) *Making Progress in Writing*. London: RoutledgeFalmer.

Bearne, E. and Warrington, M. (2003) 'Boys and writing', *Literacy Today*, 35. http://www. literacytrust.org.uk/Pubs/bearne.html (accessed 12 May 2006).

Beckett, S. (2008) *Crossover Fiction: Global and Historical Perspectives*. London: Routledge.

Becta (2002) *ImpaCT2 – Pupils' and Teachers' Perceptions of ICT in the Home, School and Community*. Coventry: Becta. http://partners.becta.org.uk/upload-dir/downloads/ page_documents/research/ImpaCT2_strand_2_report.pdf

Becta (2004) *What the Research Says about Interactive Whiteboards*. Coventry: Becta. http://publications.teachernet.gov.uk/eOrderingDownload/15006MIG2793.pdf

Benton, M. and Fox, G. (1985) *Teaching Literature 9–14*. Oxford: Oxford University Press.

Berninger, V.W. (1994) *Reading and Writing Acquisition: A Developmental Neuropsychological Perspective*. Dubuque, IA: Brown and Benchmark.

Berninger, V.W. and Graham, S. (1998) 'Language by hand: a synthesis of a decade of research on handwriting', *Handwriting Review*, 12: 11–25.

Berninger, V.W., Mizokawa, D.T. and Bragg, R. (1991) 'Theory-based diagnosis and remediation of writing disabilities', *Journal of Educational Psychology*, 29: 57–9.

Berninger, V., Vaughan, K., Abbott, R., Begay, K., Byrd, K., Curtin, G., Minnich, J. and Graham, S. (2002) 'Teaching spelling and composition alone and together: implications for the simple view of writing', *Journal of Educational Psychology*, 94: 291–304.

Bettelheim, B. (1975) *The Uses of Enchantment*. London: Penguin.

Bettelheim, B. and Zelan, K. (1981) *On Learning to Read*. London: Penguin.

Black, P.J. and Wiliam, D. (1998) *Inside the Black Box: Raising Standards Through Classroom Assessment*. London: NFER-Nelson.

Black, P. and Wiliam, D. (2003) *Assessment for Learning: Putting it into Practice*. Glasgow: Open University Press.

Browne, A. (1993) *Helping Children to Write*. London: Sage.

Bruce, T. (2009) *Learning Through Play – Babies, Toddlers and the Foundation Years* (2nd edn). London: Hodder & Stoughton Educational.

Bruner, J.S. (1966) *Toward a Theory of Instruction*. Cambridge, MA: Belknap Press.

Bruner, J.S. (1975) 'The ontogenesis of speech acts', *Journal of Child Language*, 2: 1–19.

Bruner, J. (1976) *Actual Minds, Possible Worlds*. Cambridge, MA: Harvard University Press.

Bruner, J. (1978) 'The role of dialogue in language acquisition', in A. Sinclair, R. Jarvella and W. Levelt (eds), *The Child's Conception of Language*. New York: Springer-Verlag.

Bruner, J. (1986) *Actual Minds, Possible Worlds*. Cambridge, MA: Harvard University Press.

Bruner, J. (1990) *Acts of Meaning*. Cambridge, MA: Harvard University Press.

Burkard, T. (1999) *The End of Illiteracy? The Holy Grail of Clackmannanshire*. London: Centre for Policy Studies.

Bussis, A.E., Chittenden, E.A., Amarel, M. and Klausner, E. (1985) *Inquiry into Meaning: An Investigation of Learning to Read*. Hillsdale, NJ: Erlbaum.

Byron, T. (2008) *Safer Children in a Digital World*. London: DCSF. http://www.dcsf.gov. uk/byronreview/

Carpenter, H. (1985) *Secret Gardens*. London: Allen and Unwin.

Carr, W. and Kemmis, S. (1997) *Becoming Critical: Education, Knowledge and Action Research*. London: Falmer Press.

Chall, J.S. (1983) *Learning to Read: The Great Debate*. New York: McGraw-Hill.

Chomsky, N. (1957) *Syntactic Structures*. Berlin: Mouton de Gruyter.

Chomsky, N. (1959) 'A review of B.F. Skinner's verbal behaviour', *Language*, 35(1): 26–58.

Chomsky, N. (1965) *Aspects of the Theory of Syntax*. Cambridge, MA: MIT Press.

Christensen, C.A. (2004) 'The relationship between orthographic-motor integration and computer use for the production of creative and well structured written text', *British Journal of Educational Psychology*, 74(4): 551–65.

Christensen, C.A. (2005) 'The role of orthographic-motor integration in the production of creative and well structured written text for students in secondary school', *Educational Psychology*, 25(5): 441–53.

Clark, C. and Dugdale, G. (2009) *Young People's Writing: Attitudes, Behaviour and the Role of Technology*. London: NLT.

Clay, M. (1979) *The Early Detection of Reading Difficulties*. London: Heinemann.

Clay, M. (1985) *The Early Detection of Reading Difficulties* (3rd edn). Auckland: Heinemann.

Clay, M. (1990a) *What Did I Write?* Oxford: Heinemann.

Clay, M. (1990b) *Biks and Gutches*. New York: Heinemann.

Cohen, M. (1995) *Lewis Carroll: A Biography*. London: Vintage.

Connelly, V., Gee, D. and Walsh, E. (2007) 'A comparison of keyboarded and handwritten compositions and the relationship with transcription speed', *British Journal of Educational Psychology*, 77(2): 479–92.

Conteh, J., Martin, P. and Robertson, L.H. (eds) (2007) *Multilingual Learning Stories in Britain*. Stoke-on-Trent: Trentham Books.

Cook, D. and Finlayson, H. (1999) *Interactive Children, Communicative Teaching: ICT and Classroom Teaching*. Buckingham: Open University Press.

Corbett, P. (2005) *How to Teach Fiction Writing at Key Stage 2*. Oxford: David Fulton.

Corson, D. (1988) *Oral Language across the Curriculum*. Clevedon: Multilingual Matters.

Cremin, T. (2006) 'Creativity, uncertainty and discomfort: teachers as writers', *Cambridge Journal of Education*, 36(3): 415–33.

Cremin, T., Goouch, K., Blakemore, L., Goff, E. and Macdonald, R. (2006) 'Connecting drama and writing: seizing the moment to write', *Research in Drama Education*, 11(3): 273–91.

Cremin, T.M., Mottram, M., Collins, F. and Powell, S. (2008) *Building Communities of Readers*. Leicester: UKLA Ideas in Practice Series.

Cripps, C. (1988) *A Hand for Spelling*. Cambridge: LDA Publications.

Cripps, C. and Cox, R. (1989) *Joining the ABC: How and Why Handwriting and Spelling Should Be Taught Together*. Cambridge: LDA Publications.

Crystal, D. (2006) *How Language Works*. London: Penguin.

Cummins, J. (1984) *Bilingualism and Special Education: Issues in Assessment and Pedagogy*. Clevedon: Multilingual Matters.

Cummins, J. (2000) *Language, Power and Pedagogy: Bilingual Children in the Crossfire*. Clevedon: Multilingual Matters.

Cummins, J. and Swain, M. (1986) *Bilingualism and Education*. London: Longman.

Cutler, L. and Graham, S. (2008) 'Primary grade writing instruction: a national survey', *Journal of Educational Psychology*, 100: 907–19.

Darling-Hammond, L. and Bransford, J. (eds) (2005) *Preparing Teachers for a Changing World*. San Francisco, CA: Jossey-Bass.

DCSF (2007) *Improving Writing with a Focus on Guided Writing*. London: DCSF.

DCSF (2008a) *Support for Writing*. London: The National Strategies, Primary, DCSF.

DCSF (2008b) *Talk for Writing*. London: The National Strategies, Primary, DCSF.

DCSF (2009a) *National Curriculum Assessments at Key Stage 2 in England (Provisional)*. London: DCSF.

DCSF (2009b) *Report of the Expert Group on Assessment.* London: DCSF. http://publications.dcsf.gov.uk/eOrderingDownload/Expert-Group-Report.pdf

Deacon, T. (1997) *The Symbolic Species: The Co-Evolution of Language and the Human Brain*. London: Penguin Books.

Department of Education Western Australia (DEWA) (1999) *First Steps.* Perth: Western Australian Department of Education.

DES (1965) *The Organisation of Secondary Education* (Circular 10/65). London: Department of Education and Science.

DES (1975) *A Language for Life* (Bullock Report). London: HMSO.

DfEE (1989) *National Literacy Strategy*, London: HMSO.

DfEE (2000) *Grammar for Writing*. London: DfEE.

Department for Education and Employment (DfEE) and Qualifications and Curriculum Authority (QCA) (2000) *The National Curriculum: Handbook for Primary Teachers in England, Key Stages 1 and 2*. London: TSO (The Stationery Office).

DfES (1989) *National Curriculum*. London: DfES.

DfEE (1997) 'Excellence in schools'. London: HMSO.

DfES (1998) *Progression in Phonics*. London: DfES.

DfES (2002) *The Children Act Report*. Nottingham: DfES.

DfES (2003) 'Excellence and Enjoyment, a strategy for primary schools', London: DfES.

DfES (2004a) *Five Year Strategy for Children and Learners: Maintaining the Excellent Progress*. London: DfES.

DfES (2004b) *Every Child matters: Change for Children*. London: Stationery Office.

DfES (2006a) *Primary Framework for Literacy and Mathematics*. London: HMSO. www.standards.dfes.gov.uk/primaryframeworks

DfES (2006b) *Primary National Strategy: Primary Framework for Literacy and Mathematics*. Ref: 02011-2006BOK-EN. London: DfES. http://nationalstrategies.standards.dcsf.gov.uk/node/18415 (accessed January 2010).

DfES (2007a) *Supporting Children Learning English as an Additional Language: Guidance for Practitioners in the Early Years Foundation Stage*. Ref: 00683-2007BKT-EN. London: DfES.

DfES (2007b) *Letters and Sounds: Principles and Practice of High Quality Phonics*. London: Primary National Strategy, DfES.

Dodge, B. (1995) *Some Thoughts about WebQuests*. San Diego, CA: San Diego State University. http://webquest.sdsu.edu/about_webquests.html (see also http://webquest.org/index.php).

Donaldson, M. (1989) *Sense and Sensibility*. Reading: University of Reading.

Edwards, A.D. and Westgate, D.P. (1997) *Investigating Classroom Talk*. London: The Falmer Press.

Ehri, L.C. (1987) 'Learning to read and spell words', *Journal of Reading Behaviour*, 19: 5–31.

Eliot, T.S. (1943) 'East Coker', *Four Quartets.* New York, NY: Harcourt.

Fisher, R. (2006) 'Whose writing is it anyway? Issues of control in the teaching of writing', *Cambridge Journal of Education*, 36(2): 193–206.

Fisher, R., Myhill, D., Jones, S. and Larkin, S. (2006) *Talk to Text: Using Talk to Support Writing*. Unpublished report from the School of Education and Lifelong Learning, University of Exeter. www.education.exeter.ac.uk/download.php?id=4977

Flippo, R.F. (2005) 'Feature article: questions to consider when reviewing standardized tests for classroom use', *WSRA Journal*, 45(3): 24–5.

Flynn, N. and Stainthorp, R. (2006) *The Learning and Teaching of Reading and Writing*. Bognor Regis: John Wiley and Sons.

Fox, B. (2002) 'Talking stories, textoids and dialogic reading', in M. Monteith (ed.), *Teaching Primary Literacy with ICT*. Buckingham: Open University Press.

Fox, B. (2007) 'Digital storytelling with Photo Story 3', *Sharing Good Practice*, 12. http://www.ictopus.org.uk

Fox, R., Poulson, L., Medwell, J. and Wray, D. (2001) *Teaching Literacy Effectively in the Primary School*. London: Routledge.

Freeman, A.R., MacKinnon, J.R. and Miller, L.T. (2005) 'Keyboarding for students with handwriting problems: a literature review', *Physical and Occupational Therapy in Pediatrics*, 25(1): 119–47.

Frith, U. (1985) 'Developmental dyslexia', in K.E. Patterson, J. Marshall and M. Coltheart (eds), *Surface Dyslexia*. Hove: Erlbaum.

Galton, M., Hargreaves, L., Comber, C., Wall, D. and Pell, T. (1999) 'Changes in patterns of teacher interaction in primary classrooms 1976–1996', *British Journal of Educational Research*, 25(1): 23–35.

Gee, J.P. (2004) *Situated Language Learning: A Critique of Traditional Schooling*. Abingdon: Routledge.

Goodman, K.S. (1967) 'Reading: a psycholinguistic guessing game', *Journal of the Reading Specialist*, 4: 126–35.

Goodman, K.S. (1973) 'Psycholinguistic universals in the reading process', in F. Smith (ed.), *Psycholinguistics and Reading*. New York: Holt, Rinehart and Winston.

Goodman, K.S. (1996) *On Reading*. Portsmouth, NH: Heinemann.

Goodman, Y., Watson, D. and Burke, C. (1987) *Reading Miscue Inventory*. New York: Richard Owen.

Goodwin, P. (2005) *The Literate Classroom*. London: David Fulton.

Goodwin, P. (2006) *The Literate Classroom* (2nd edn). London: Routledge.

Goouch, K. and Lambirth, A. (2007) 'Introduction: sound and fury', in K. Goouch and A. Lambirth (eds), *Understanding Phonics and the Teaching of Reading: Critical Perspectives*. Maidenhead: Open University Press.

Goswami, U. (2007) 'Learning to read across languages: the role of phonics and synthetic phonics', in K. Goouch and A. Lambirth (eds), *Understanding Phonics and the Teaching of Reading: Critical Perspectives*. Maidenhead: Open University Press.

Gough, P.B. and Hillinger, M.L. (1980) 'Learning to read: an unnatural act', *Bulletin of the Orton Society*, 30: 179–96.

Gough, P.B. and Tunmer, W.E. (1986) 'Decoding, reading and reading disability', *Remedial and Special Education*, 7: 6–10.

Graham, S., Berninger, V., Abbott, R., Abbott, S. and Whitaker, D. (1997) 'The role of mechanics in composing of elementary school students: a new methodological approach', *Journal of Educational Psychology*, 89(1): 170–82.

Gravelle, M. (ed.) (2000) *Planning for Bilingual Learners: An Inclusive Curriculum*. Stock-on-Trent: Trentham Books.

Graves, D.H. (1983) *Writing: Teachers & Children at Work*. London: Heinemann Educational Books.

Gregory, E., Long, S. and Volk, D. (2004) *Many Pathways to Literacy*. London: RoutledgeFalmer.

Hall, K. (2003) *Listening to Stephen Read: Multiple Perspectives on Literacy*. Buckingham: Open University Press.

Halliday, M.A.K. (1975) *Learning How to Mean*. London: Edward Arnold.

Halliday, M.A.K. (1985) *An Introduction to Functional Grammar*. London: Edward Arnold.

Halliday, M.A.K. (1987) *New Developments in Systemic Linguistics*. London: Pinter.

Hawkins, D. (1973) in Armstrong, M. (2010) 'Two sources of learning', *Forum for the Discussion of New Trends in Education*, 16(1): Autumn, 1973.

Hennessy, S., Deaney, R., Ruthven, K. and Winterbottom, M. (2007) 'Pedagogical strategies for using the interactive whiteboard to foster learner participation in school science', *Learning Media and Technology*, 32(3): 283–301.

Hofkins, D. and Northen, S. (eds) (2009) *Introducing the Cambridge Primary Review*. London: Routledge.

Holdaway, D. (1979) *The Foundations of Literacy*. NSW: Ashton Scholastic.

Holdaway, D. (1980) *Independence in Reading*. NSW: Ashton Scholastic.

Hunt, P. (1994) *An Introduction to Children's Literature*. Oxford: Oxford University Press.

Hunt, P. (1995) *Children's Literature: An Illustrated History*. Oxford: Oxford University Press.

Hynds, J. (2007) 'Putting the Spin on Reading: The Language of the Rose Review', *Journal of Early Childhood Literacy*, 7(3): 267–81.

Johnston, R. and Watson, J. (2003) *Accelerating Reading and Spelling with Synthetic Phonics: A Five Year Follow Up*. Edinburgh: Scottish Executive Department, Insight 4.

Johnston, R. and Watson, J. (2005) *The Effects of Synthetic Phonics Teaching on Reading and Spelling Attainment: A Seven-Year Longitudinal Study*. http://www.scotland.gov.uk/Resource/Doc/36496/0023582.pdf (accessed December 2006).

Johnston, R. and Watson, J. (2007) *Teaching Synthetic Phonics*. Exeter: Learning Matters.

Jones, D. (2004) 'Automaticity of the transcription process in the production of written text'. Unpublished Doctor of Philosophy thesis, University of Queensland, Australia.

Jones, D. and Christensen, C. (1999) 'The relationship between automaticity in handwriting and students' ability to generate written text', *Journal of Educational Psychology*, 91: 44–9.

Jones, P. (1988) *Lip-service: The Story of Talk in Schools*. Milton Keynes: Open University Press.

Keating, I., Robertson, C., Roberts, I. and Shenton, L. (1996) 'Policy documents: on the wall or in the waste bin?', *Reading*, 30(3): 37–40.

Kenner, C. (2004) 'Living in simultaneous worlds: difference and integration in bilingual script-learning'. *International Journal of Bilingual Education and Bilingualism*, 7(1): 43–61.

Kingston University (2006) *Books Alive!* http://www.kingston.ac.uk/booksalive/progress.html

Kress, G. (1994) *Learning to Write*. Oxford: Routledge.

Kress, G. (2003) *Literacy in the New Media Age*. London: Routledge.

Lambirth, A. (2006) *Planning Creative Literacy Lessons*. London: Routledge.

Larson, J. and Marsh, J. (2005) *Making Literacy Real: Theories and Practices for Learning*. London: Sage.

Latham, D. (2002) *How Children Learn to Write: Supporting and Developing Children's Writing in School*. London: Paul Chapman Publishing.

Lave, J. and Wenger, E. (1991) *Situated Learning: Legitimate Peripheral Participation*. Cambridge: Cambridge University Press.

Lewis, D. (2001) *Reading Contemporary Picturebooks: Picturing Text*. London: Routledge.

Lewis, R. (1998) 'Enhancing the writing of students with disabilities through technology: an investigation of the effects of text entry tools, editing tools, and speech synthesis'. Final report for H1800G40073, Special Education programs, Washington, DC.

Macnair, L., Evans, S., Perkins, M. and Goodwin, P. (2006) 'Inside the classroom: three approaches to phonics teaching', in M. Lewis and S. Ellis (eds), *Phonics: Practice, Research and Policy*. London: Paul Chapman Publishing.

Marsh, J. and Millard, E. (2000) *Literacy and Popular Culture: Using Children's Culture in the Classroom*. London: Paul Chapman Publishing.

Marsh, J., Brooks, G., Hughes, J., Ritchie, L., Roberts, S. and Wright, K. (2005) *Digital Beginnings: Young Children's Use of Popular Culture, Media and New Technologies*. Sheffield: University of Sheffield. http://www.esmeefairbairn.org.uk/docs/Digital BeginningsReport.pdf

Maun, I. and Myhill, D.A. (2005) 'Text as design, writers as designers', *English in Education,* 39(2): 5–21.

McPake, J., Stephen, C., Plowman, L., Sime, D. and Downey, S. (2004) *Already at a Disadvantage? ICT in the Home and Children's Preparation for Primary School. Final Report to BECTA*. University of Stirling: Institute of Education. http://www.ioe. stir.ac.uk/research/projects/interplay/docs/already_at_a_disadvantage.pdf

Medwell, J. (forthcoming) *The Teaching of Handwriting in England. A Three-year Survey*.

Medwell, J. and Wray, D. (2007) 'Handwriting: what do we know and what do we need to know?', *Literacy,* 41(1): 10–15.

Medwell, J., Strand, S. and Wray, D. (2007) 'The role of handwriting in composing for Y2 children', *Journal of Reading, Writing and Literacy*, 2(1): 18–36.

Medwell, J., Strand, S. and Wray, D. (2009) 'The links between handwriting and composing for Y6 children', *Cambridge Journal of Education*, 39(3): 329–44.

Meek, M. (1982) *Learning to Read.* London: Bodley Head.

Meek, M. (1988) *How Texts Teach What Readers Learn.* Stroud: Thimble Press.

Meek, M., Warlow, A. and Barton, G. (1977) *The Cool Web*. London: Bodley Head.

Mercer, N. (1995) *The Guided Construction of Knowledge: Talk Amongst Teachers and Learners*. Clevedon: Multilingual Matters.

Mercer, N. (2000) *Words and Minds: How we Use Language to Think Together.* London: Routledge.

Mercer, N. and Littleton, K. (2007) *Dialogue and the Development of Children's Thinking: A Socio-cultural Approach*. Oxford: Routledge.

Mercer, N., Wegerif, R. and Dawes, L. (1999) 'Children's talk and the development of reasoning in the classroom', *British Journal of Educational Research*, 25(1): 95–111.

Morris, D., Ervin, C. and Conrad, K. (1996) 'A case study of middle school reading disability in teaching struggling readers', *The Reading Teacher*, 49(5): 368–77.

Mullis, I.V.S., Martin, M.O., Olson, J.F., Berger, D.R. Milne, D. and Stanco, G.M. (eds) (2008) *TIMSS 2007 Encyclopedia: A Guide to Mathematics and Science Education Around the World, Vol. 2 M-Z and Benchmarking Participants*. Chestnut Hill, MA: Boston College.

Mursepp, M. (2005) *The Sunny Side of Darkness: Children's Literature in Totalitarian and Post-totalitarian Eastern Europe*. Tallin: University of Tallinn Press.

Myhill, D. (2001) 'Writing: creating and crafting', *English in Education*, 35(3): 13–20.

Myhill, D. and Dunkin, F. (2002) 'What's a good question?', *Literacy Today* 33.

Myhill, D. and Fisher, R.J. (2006) '*Informing Practice: A Review of Research in Literacy and the Teaching of English*. Commissioned literature review for Ofsted, HMI 2531. http://www.collaborativelearning.org/speakingandlistening.html/ (accessed 10 February 2010).

Myhill, D. and Jones, S. (2009) 'How talk becomes text: investigating the concept of oral rehearsal in early years' classrooms', *British Journal of Educational Studies*, 57(3): 265–84.

National Strategies/DCSF (2008) *Improving Writing, with a Particular Focus on Supporting Boys' Writing Development*. London: National Strategies/DCSF. http:// nationalstrategies.standards.dcsf.gov.uk/node/18092 (accessed 22 February 2010).

Nodelman, P. (1972) *The Pleasure of Children's Literature*. White Plains, NY: Longman.

Ofsted (2005) *English 2000–2005: A Review of Inspection Evidence*. London: Ofsted.

Ofsted (2008) *Inspecting English as an Additional Language*. http://www.naldic.org.uk/docs/resources/documents/SchoolsandInspection06ExtractInspectingEnglishasanAdditionalLanguage.pdf

Ofsted (2009) *English at the Crossroads*. London: Ofsted.

Organisation for Economic Co-operation and Development (OECD) (2000) *Programme for International Student Assessment (PISA)*. http://www.oecd.org/dataoecd/44/28/1894907.pdf

Pascal, C. and Bertram, A.D. (eds) (1997) *Effective Early Learning: Case Studies of Improvement*. London: Hodder and Stoughton.

Perfetti, C.K. and McCutchen, D. (1987) 'Schooled language competence: linguistic abilities in reading and writing', in S. Rosenberg (ed.), *Advances in Applied Psycholinguistics*. Vol. 2. Cambridge: Cambridge University Press.

Peters, M. (1985) *Spelling Caught or Taught: A New Look*. London: Routledge and Kegan Paul.

Peters, M. and Smith, B. (1993) *Spelling in Context*. Slough: NFER Nelson.

Piaget, J. (1970) *The Science of Education and the Psychology of the Child*. New York: Viking.

Popham, W.J. (2009) 'Assessment literacy for teachers: faddish or fundamental?', *Theory Into Practice*, 48: 4–11.

Prensky, M. (2001) 'Digital natives, digital immigrants', *On the Horizon*, 9(5). http://www.marcprensky.com/writing/default.asp

Primary National Strategy (2007) *Letters and Sounds*. http://www.standards.dfes.gov.uk/clld/las.html (accessed December 2007).

Qualification and Curriculum Authority (QCA) (2005) *National Curriculum in Action: Creativity*. London: QCA.

Qualifications and Curriculum Authority (QCA) (2008) *Assessing Pupil's Progress: Assessment at the Heart of Learning*. London: QCA.

Qualifications and Curriculum Development Agency (QCDA) (2010) *National Curriculum*. http://curriculum.qcda.gov.uk/new-primary-curriculum/areas-of-learning/understanding-English-communication-and-languages/programme-of-learning/index.aspx?tab=6 (accessed 1 February 2010).

Quayle, E. (1971) *The Collectors Book of Books*. London: Studio Vista.

Reynolds, K. (2007) *Radical Children's Literature: Future Visions and Aesthetic Transformations in Juvenile Fiction*. Basingstoke: Palgrave.

Reynolds, K. and Tucker, N. (eds) (1998) *Children's Book Publishing in Britain since 1945*. Aldershot: Scolar/Ashgate.

Robinson, K. (2009) *The Element: How Finding your Passion Changes Everything*. London: Penguin Books.

Robertson, C. (1995) 'Children and story in the primary school'. Unpublished Masters thesis, Manchester Metropolitan University library.

Robertson, C., Keating, I., Roberts, I. and Shenton, L. (1996) 'Uninterrupted sustained silent reading: the rhetoric and the practice', *The Journal of Research in Reading*, 19(1): 25–35.

Rogoff, B. (1990) *Apprenticeship in Thinking: Cognitive Development in a Social Context*. New York: Oxford University Press.

Rogoff, B., Goodman-Turkanis, C. and Bartlett, L. (2001) *Learning Together: Children and Adults in a School Community*. Oxford: Oxford University Press.

Rose, J. (2006) *Independent Review of the Teaching of Early Reading*. Nottingham: DfES Publications.

Rose, J. (2009) *Independent Review of the Primary Curriculum: Final Report*. Nottingham: DCSF Publications. http://publications.education.gov.uk/Primary_curriculum_Report.pdf

Sassoon, R. (1990) *Handwriting: A New Perspective*. Cheltenham: Stanley Thornes.

Sassoon, R. (1993) *The Art and Science of Handwriting*. Bristol: Intellect.

Sharples, M. (1999) *How We Write: Writing as Creative Design*. London: Routledge.

Smith, F. (1971) *Understanding Reading: A Psycholinguistic Analysis of Reading and Learning to Read*. New York: Holt, Rinehart and Winston.

Smith, F. (1982) *Writing and the Writer*. London: Heinemann.

Smith, F. (1984) *Writing and the Writer*. London: Heinemann.

Smith, F., Hardman, F. and Higgins, S. (2006) 'The impact of interactive whiteboards on teacher-pupil interaction in the National Literacy and Numeracy Strategies', *British Education Research Journal*, 32(3): 443–57.

Snow, C.E., Burns, S. and Griffin, P. (eds) (1998) *Preventing Reading Difficulties in Young Children*. National Academy Press: Washington, DC.

Somekh, B., Haldene, M., Jones, K., Lewin, C., Steadman, S., Scrimshaw, P., Sing, S., Bird, K., Cummings, J., Downing, B., Harber Stuart, T., Jarvis, J., Mavers, D. and Woodrew, D. (2007) *Evaluation of the Primary Schools Whiteboard Expansion Project*. London: DfES.

Stables, A. (2003) 'Learning, identity and classroom dialogue', *Journal of Educational Enquiry*, 4(1): 440–6.

Stainthorp, R. (2002) 'Writing is hard', *Psychology of Education Review*, 26: 3–11.

Stanovich, K.E. (1992) 'The psychology of reading: evolutionary and revolutionary developments', *Annual Review of Applied Linguistics*, 12: 3–30.

Stephens, J. (1992) *Language and Ideology in Children's Fiction*. White Plains, NY: Longman.

Street, B. (1984) *Literacy in Theory and Practice*. New York: Cambridge University Press.

Street, B. and Street, J. (1991) 'The schooling of literacy', in D. Barton and R. Ivanics (eds), *Writing in the Community*. London: Sage.

Styles, M. and Drummond, M.J. (1993) 'The politics of reading', *Cambridge Journal of Education*, 23(1): 3–13.

Tann, S. (1991) *Developing Language in the Primary Classroom*. London: Cassell.

Taylor, J. (2001) *Handwriting: A Teacher's Guide*. Abingdon: David Fulton.

Tolkein, J.R.R. (1964) *Tree and Leaf*. Cambridge: Canto.

Torgesen, J., Wagner, R., Rashotte, C. and Herron, J. (2003) 'Summary of outcomes from first grade study with Read, Write, and Type and Auditory Discrimination in Depth instruction and software with at-risk children'. FCRR Tech. Ref. No. 2. Retrieved from Florida Center for Reading Research. http://www.fcrr.org/technicalReports/RWTfullrept.pdf

Townsend, J.R. (1965) *Written for Children*. London: Scarecrow.

Training and Development Agency for Schools. (TDA) (2007) *Professional Standards for Teachers*. London: TDA.

Training and Development Agency for Schools (TDA) (2009) *One to One Tuition Programme*. http://www.tda.gov.uk/teachers/onetoonetuition.aspx

Tucker, N. (ed.) (1976) *Suitable for Children?* Sussex University Press.

UKLA (2010) 'UKLA launches its vision for future literacy education', Tuesday, April 20, 2010, http://www.ukla.org/news/

Vygotsky, L.S. (1928) *Thought and Language*. New York: Wiley.

Vygotsky, L.S. (1962) *Language and Thought*. Cambridge, MA: Harvard University Press.

Vygotsky, L.S. (1978) *Mind and Society*. Cambridge, MA: Harvard University Press.

Watson, V. (1996) 'Power and freedom in children's reading', *Literacy*, 27(3): 45–50.

Webb, J. and Cox, R. (2010) Keynote address to 'Children's Literature and its Impact on Improving Writing Skills' Conference. The Courtyard Theatre, Hereford, January 26, 2010.

Wells, G. (1986) *The Meaning Makers*. London: Hodder and Stoughton.

Wiley, T.L. (2005) *Literacy and Language Diversity in the United States* (2nd edn). Centre for Applied Linguistics: McHenry, Illinois.

Wilkie-Stibbs, C. (2002) *The Feminine Subject in Children's Literature*. New York: Routledge.

Wilkinson, A. (1980) *Assessing Language Development*. Oxford: Oxford University Press.

Wolfe, S. and Alexander, R. (2008) *Argumentation and Dialogic Thinking: Alternative Pedagogies for a Changing World*. www.beyondcurrenthorizons.org.uk (accessed 15 February 2010).

Wray, D. (1993) 'What do children think about writing?', *Educational Review*, 45(1): 67–77.

Wray, D. and Lewis, M. (1997) *Extending Literacy: Children Reading and Writing Non Fiction*. London: Routledge.

Wyse, D. and Goswami, U. (2008) 'Synthetic phonics and the teaching of reading', *British Educational Research Journal*, 34(6): 691–710.

Wyse, D. and Styles, M. (2007) 'Synthetic phonics and the teaching of reading: the debate surrounding England's "Rose Report"', *Literacy*, 41(1): 35–42.

Zipes, J. (1979) *Breaking the Magic Spell: Radical Theories of Folk and Fairy Tales*. Lexington, KY: University Press of Kentucky.

INDEX